**Cooking Lessons
Tales from the Kitchen
and Other Stories**

Cooking Lessons

Tales from the Kitchen and Other Stories

Daisy Garnett

Illustrations by Carmen Carreira

Quadrille

For my parents, and in
celebration of Cannwood.

Editorial Director Jane O'Shea
Creative Director Helen Lewis
Project Editor Laura Herring
Designer Claire Peters
Illustrator Carmen Carreira
Production Denise Stone

First published in 2008 by
Quadrille Publishing Limited,
Alhambra House, 27-31 Charing Cross Road
London WC2H 0LS
www.quadrille.co.uk

Text © 2008 Daisy Garnett, except for pages
42, 88–9, 99–100, 101, 102–3, 108–9, 133,
148–9, 161, 194, see page 224 for details
Illustrations © 2008 Carmen Carreira
Design and layout © 2008 Quadrille Publishing
Limited

Cataloguing in Publication Data: a catalogue
record for this book is available from the
British Library.

ISBN 978 184400 615 1

Printed in China

Chapter one
Why I cook.
And the summer of
pine nut ice cream

Why I cook

My sister (I am lucky enough to have two) Rose has just returned from Rome – a half-term trip with her two small sons, George and Frankie, her husband Tom and a friend of all of ours (an adopted brother more or less) called Will. The trip was very much a success.

'I ate the best pizza in the world,' she says to me on the telephone, immediately on her return.

'Of course you did,' I reply. 'You were in Rome.'

'Yes,' she says, 'but even by Rome standards it was something else.' She pauses. She knows she has my full attention. 'That wasn't the only thing,' she says, then pauses again. I can hear her silently remembering the other thing.

'Yes?' I respond.

'A discovery,' she says. 'But you probably already know about it.'

'Probably, but what is it?'

'Pine nut ice cream,' she says, letting the words hang between us.

'Really?' I ask. 'That good?'

'Oh my God, Daise. Better. Like nothing-you've-ever-eaten good. You've never had it? Nor had I. Will ordered it. I never would, would you?'

Rose continues to talk like this about the ice cream experience. She is doing it more for my sake than hers, but even so I only half listen. Mostly I am thinking: 'Well, it makes sense: think of pistachio ice cream or hazelnut, only with pine nuts. You'd toast them first. And make a paste, probably sweetened with honey. Could it really be better than pistachio ice cream, though? The novelty adds something of course; the surprise'. Then I think: 'Do I have time to try to make it this afternoon. How many pine nuts do I have? Do I have cream for the custard base? Can I start now or do I have to ask more questions about Rome?'

'I wonder,' Rose says, her tone changing from reverie to pointed curiosity, 'how easy it would be to make? That's by the by though. The point is, next time you're in Italy, pine nut ice cream. That's my tip.'

My sister doesn't have to say anything else. She knows that soon, when it is hot, and we are all together in Somerset, where we grew up and where my parents still live, and where there is a garden and an ice cream maker, she will be eating pine nut ice

8

cream again. I will serve it without fuss or announcement, so that she and any others around the table (and usually there are ten or twelve) will welcome it well enough as vanilla. But it won't be vanilla. It will be pine nut. And the end of lunch will be lifted by that fact alone, never mind how good the ice cream may actually be. A little bit of Rome will have made it into the meal, we will laugh, and I will take some shit for obsessively having had to reproduce it. Will anyone really care whether I serve pine nut ice cream instead of vanilla? Of course not. But why not snatch a little bit of Rome to enjoy on a Somerset afternoon? Why not, for me, fess up to obsessiveness? Why not, for them, indulge in it?

I cook as much as I can for all kinds of reasons: because it needs doing, because I enjoy it, because I am interested in what it reveals about our values and history and culture and environment and economy, our fads and our fashions, and the easiest way to understand more about all this is by doing it oneself. But I also spend time and take care cooking because it produces instant, often alchemical results around a table. It produces food, of course, but also a sense of ritual and a reason to celebrate our everyday good fortune in being able to sit down together – or just sit down alone, and feed ourselves.

Have you ever made Omelette Arnold Bennett for someone? Try it. I swear the only thing that beats sharing this unbelievable delicacy is cooking it first. I don't want food to stand in for love or intimacy, or to be used to relieve boredom or anxiety (although it has done all of those things for me at one point or another) but I do think – and this is hardly a revelation – that a meal eaten together can help with all those things. What was a surprise to me was how much the actual process of cooking, this meditative, often rhythmic, sometimes frustrating, occasionally challenging, deeply satisfying and rewarding activity, helps, too.

Omelette Arnold Bennett

This omelette – so the story goes – was created by the Savoy Hotel in the 1920s, for the novelist and critic Arnold Bennett to eat when he dined at the hotel after an evening at the theatre, which he did frequently. This recipe serves two more than generously, three absolutely adequately, and four perfectly well. A green salad and a loaf of bread would be the only other things required.

You need 100g of **undyed smoked haddock** (remove its skin) and enough **milk** (full-fat) to cover it when it is sitting snugly in a saucepan. Simmer the haddock in the milk until it is cooked, which will take about ten minutes. You'll know it is done when it separates into flakes easily.

Drain away the milk, and put 100ml **cream** and a knob of **butter** (10-15g) into the saucepan with the haddock. Stir it all together gently for a minute or two over a moderate heat, so that the haddock breaks up and is warmed through with the cream and butter.

Separate four free-range **eggs** and beat the yolks with a tablespoon of cream. Season with **salt** and freshly ground **black pepper**. Mix the yolks with the haddock.

Whip the egg whites until they are fairly stiff, so that they are just able to stand in peaks, but would still fall out of the bowl if you tipped it up.

Grate two tablespoons of **Parmesan** and mix in with the egg yolk, haddock, and cream. Fold the egg whites gently into this mixture.

Preheat your grill. Melt another similar-sized knob of butter in a large non-stick ovenproof frying pan and heat it until it foams. Pour the omelette mix into the pan and let it cook on a medium heat until the base is golden and it has just set. Spoon a little more cream (or leave it off if you don't fancy it being quite so rich) and another tablespoon of Parmesan onto the omelette. Take it off the heat and put it under the hot grill. It will rise, so that it is puffy, and turn a beautiful golden colour.

As soon as it has done this – it only takes a couple of minutes – whip it out from under the grill and slide it onto a hot serving plate or divide it straight from the pan onto eating plates. Sprinkle with chopped **flat-leaf parsley** and race to the table.

And now to pine nut ice cream

It took me a long time to get this recipe right, but then working it out was entirely the point. The first couple of times, I didn't sieve the pine nut custard, which meant the ice cream had a slightly chewy, bitty texture, which wasn't unpleasant, but neither was it sublime. But sieving definitely improved it. In further experiments, I nearly doubled my egg and cream count. It was delicious. Go figure. This new version – which I believe now worthy – is a gift of love to Rose.

A note on sugar thermometers: use one. They are a fail-safe way of knowing how long you need to cook the egg-custard base for. That's very important, because if you cook the custard for too long it can curdle and result in grainy ice cream. This is disappointing and must, for the sake of Cook's sanity, be avoided. An inferior ice-cream maker, with too small a motor, can be another reason for this. Ours is quite a good one, has been going for ten years and has never once misbehaved (even though I once dropped it from a great height and it nearly broke the floor). But start with a sugar thermometer; you can get them fairly cheaply at even the most basic kitchen shops.

Pine nut ice cream

125g pine nuts
150g Acacia honey (or use
   any runny, mild-flavoured
   honey)
600ml double cream
300ml full-fat milk

4 coffee beans
4 strips of orange peel (pared
   away from the fruit using a
   vegetable peeler)
7 free-range egg yolks

1 Roast the pine nuts on a baking tray in a moderate oven (180°C/350°F/gas mark 4) for 5–10 minutes, giving them a stir half-way through, until they are lightly toasted. You can toast them in a large, dry frying pan if you'd prefer, but make sure the pine nuts are in a single layer and watch them like a hawk. DO NOT LET THEM BURN. If they do, cut your losses and start again. Better to waste a cup of pine nuts than spoil seven egg yolks and a good deal of cream by ending up with bitter, burnt-tasting ice cream. (I've been there.)

2 Blend the nuts with the honey in a food processor, so that the mixture forms a smooth paste and then put this paste, together with the cream, milk, coffee beans and orange peel into a pan and heat it until just below boiling point – that is until you see bubbles just beginning to appear around the edges of the pan. Remove from the heat.

3 Whisk the egg yolks in a bowl, then pour the hot milk and cream mixture over them, and stir everything together well.

4 Wash out the saucepan you've just used, so that any burnt milk particles lingering in the bottom of the pan are banished and pour the custard back into the clean pan. Cook this mixture over a slow heat – I use a diffuser mat – stirring constantly for about ten minutes, by which point the liquid will have reached 75°C/165°F.

You will know this by using your sugar thermometer. If it hasn't reached 75°C/165°F, keep stirring and gently heating until it has. This is boring but necessary, because if the mixture gets any hotter it will curdle.

5 Once it has reached the correct temperature and thickened somewhat, take it off the heat and cool the mixture by pouring it into a bowl, preferably one sitting in iced water.

6 When it is cool put the whole mixture through a sieve, then let it sit in the fridge for half an hour, before churning it in your ice cream maker.

7 Transfer to a container that has a tight-fitting lid and freeze for three hours before serving. If you freeze it for longer, make sure you take it out half an hour or so before serving it, so it becomes soft enough to eat.

I make ice cream a lot. But then I make a lot of things in the kitchen a lot. Sometimes I wish that's all I ever did, but, like most people, I cook when I have the time, mostly in the evenings and at weekends. Okay, sometimes I make time. Sometimes I put off other things like articles that are due – okay, *particularly* articles that are due – in order to cook. I feel calm, mostly, when I cook. I feel happy and content and busy and useful. I feel 'in the moment,' and I hate that expression, but how else can I put it?

I suppose there is my friend Gordon's way. Gordon is an antique dealer in his early fifties. He is intelligent and opinionated and boisterous, ruthless when he wants to be, pedantic, too, on certain points, but exceedingly generous, filled with curiosity, and, because he reads so much, posesses a prodigious memory and a fine analytical mind. Gordon and I were in Ireland not long ago, staying with our friend Thomas, whom we both adore and who has built a modern glasshouse in the wild hills of Kerry, though he lives mostly in London. I love going to stay with

Thomas for all kinds of reasons, but one of them is that there is so much time to cook when you're there. The phone doesn't ring, you can't get email and there are few errands to run – except ones involving eating and the pub. But it's not totally isolated. Thomas has friends in the village that we meet for a drink or who sometimes join us for dinner. One of them, James, a gardener, was round helping Thomas with plans for a new vegetable garden.

'Are you into food, then?' James enquired during dinner, looking at the three of us. I expect food was all we had talked about so far. Amazingly, it didn't appear to be a rhetorical question.

'*Are we into food?*' Gordon spluttered. 'Are we into food!? This one,' he said, pointing at me, 'writes about it for a living. Thomas, as you know, is trying to grow it, and I'm obese. Yes, I think you could say we're into food.'

I am into food. Although, it wasn't always thus. Or, at least, though I have always liked eating, I used to pay less attention to what went into my mouth – as long as there was quite a lot of it. And though, occasionally, I threw some pasta into a saucepan, I rarely, if ever, cooked. Now, I spend half a summer conquering pine nut ice cream because my sister tasted it in Rome and considered it a delicacy. Now, I lie awake at night thinking: if I get up an hour earlier than everyone else then I'll have time to make *Iles Flotante* for pudding at lunch, and if no one sees me then they won't think I'm weird. Now, I read cookery books before I go to sleep and keep files and files of recipes both on paper and on my computer. One of the computer files, updated often, is called General Tips.

General Tips is where I type that a pound is equal to 455g and a pint is 565ml, a stick of butter is 120g, a cup is 225g and a tablespoon is 15g. (American cookbooks use these measurements. A cup to measure rice or sugar, I see. But sticks of butter?) It is here that I have written down: "The fresher the veg., the quicker it will cook", and, on fish: "Always ask your fishmonger to remove the membrane as well as the skin from monkfish, and ask him to include the cheeks, because then he'll know you are serious about fish and he'll give you the freshest monkfish in the shop. If you're poaching monkfish (and a chunk of monkfish is called a collop) then use one teaspoon of salt for each 1.1 litre or 2 pints of water. For salmon, make it a tablespoon."

The rules and tips that I have gathered in this file seem to be quite random. "Use cold water for stock; it draws the flavour out of the bones" leads into instructions on shrimp, which "should be lowered into heavily salted boiling water and are done when they are coral-coloured all the way through, with no sign of grey on the back." The computer also says that they freeze very well once cooked, and they do. I know this because the things written in this file are lessons that I have learnt, often in the order I have learnt them, which also explains how they fall. "The liquid from cooking the shrimp is salty but quite good", I now know. "Freeze it," I add, "for when you do a fish soup, and do the same with the shells. To use the shells break them up with a hammer. Toast them in olive oil, white wine, a dash of brandy, a tin of tomatoes, carrots, onion and a bouquet garni and simmer for a long time, then pass through a sieve. But simmer a fish stock that uses bones and heads – halibut and turbot being ideal – for 30 minutes only. Any longer and the bones will break down so much it will become bitter."

"Walnut oil: keep in fridge." "Brandy Butter: use the food processor. It will make it wonderfully light." "New potatoes go into boiling salted water, whereas for making mash put the potatoes, with their skin on (to keep water out) in cold water and bring up to the boil, then peel the potatoes once they are cooked." "When braising, the meat must first be sealed. Braise in an inch of liquid. Stewing requires meat to be almost covered." "A simmer is a definite bubble." And so on. And on. And on…

I didn't properly cook until I was thirty, when I found myself to be the only non-sailor on a small boat, sailing across the Atlantic Ocean with four friends. I realised that making sandwiches every day for two months at sea was not going to cut it. I thought, before I had tried doing it, that cooking was a chore. But I discovered that it didn't have to be something I couldn't do. I *could* do it. Anyone can. Over the page, for example, is how to make a simple supper of infinite deliciousness.

Grilled lamb chops and a green salad

Buy two or three or four **lamb chops**, or however many you need, preferably from a good butcher. You can either buy a thick chop from the loin or a smaller, daintier cutlet, which comes from the best end of neck. Which you choose depends on what you feel like eating: something substantial and chunkier that requires a sharp knife and fork, or something more delicate and less filling that you can pick up with your fingers and do away with in one or two bites?

Enhance the meat by adding some flavour. Lamb itself has a strong taste that you don't want to mask, but it suits being matched with other robust flavours such as rosemary, thyme and garlic – anchovy, too, very well. Crush a clove or two of **garlic** with the blade of a wide knife, sprinkle it with a little **salt** and, using the edge of the knife to continue crushing it, make it into a paste. You will also need some freshly ground **black pepper** and a good sprinkling of **herbes de province** – a mixture of herbs that should contain (and it's worth checking) rosemary, thyme, basil, fennel seed, lavender, marjoram, sage and summer savoury – the very things that a lamb living a pretty nice life in the hills of southern France might be living on. Lay the chops out and rub a little crushed garlic, black pepper and a sprinkling of herbes de province into one side.

Heat the grill until it's really hot. It's easier to use the grill element in your oven for lamb chops rather than a grill pan on top of the hob because lamb chops are fatty and if you put them on a rack suspended over an oven tray (line it with aluminium foil to save on washing up), the fat has somewhere to drip onto. Cook them under the hot grill for ten minutes for a thick chop, much less for a thinner cutlet. I like my chops very pink inside, so it might be as little as two or three minutes on each side, depending on their size and thickness. The only way to really know how you like them is by experimenting. Turn the chops over, using a pair of tongs, and sprinkle the new up-turned side with more garlic, pepper and herbes de province. Put them back under the grill for a little less time than the first side. About six minutes for loin chops, two or three minutes for cutlets. Chops should be eaten immediately.

A good green salad

Beans, whether they are French green beans, haricots verts or white beans all go very well with lamb (as do any greens). So, too, do aubergines, tomatoes and, of course, potatoes – potatoes dauphinoise being a particularly good match. But, for the simplest supper, a good loaf of bread – you want it to soak up any juices – and a green, well-dressed salad is more than ample accompaniment.

A green salad should be made with care. In summer, the garden or markets are full of things to put into a green salad: soft butter lettuces, chickweed, lambs lettuce, the smaller leaves from broad beans, peas and beetroot, rocket and sorrel, as well as fresh herbs. I love sprigs of parsley and chervil and small basil leaves in my salad. In winter it is harder to source such a variety of ingredients, but not impossible. Think about adding the smaller leaves from brussel sprout tops (steam or boil the larger ones and dress with a little lemon and olive oil), fennel sliced as thinly as possible across the bulb, small cavolo nero leaves and the tips of sprouting broccoli. Watercress is available all year round and so are endive and spinach (use the small leaves or baby spinach).

You can use either a selection of leaves (combine sweet leaves with more bitter ones for a balance) or keep to one variety of green, though bear in mind that what you choose then must be delicious and interesting enough not to need any company. In summer when the pale green soft butter lettuces are plentiful I often make a salad using nothing but them and a few parsley or chervil leaves. They need only the lightest of dressings their taste and texture is so magnificent. But this luxury does not always avail itself.

Lettuce needs to be clean and dry. Rose hates this job more than any other. 'Why?' I asked her once. 'Because it's REALLY BORING,' she shouted back, and she's right, but it is also really essential. Grit or dirt in a salad is ruinous. Wash the leaves in a bowl of cold water (don't leave them to soak, or they will go limp), swirling them about, then dry them either in a salad spinner or by laying them out to drain on a clean tea towel, then blotting them with another tea towel or some kitchen paper. The salad spinner is by far the quickest and easiest route, though even then a bit of a blot doesn't go amiss.

Now for the dressing

I usually make the dressing straight into the salad bowl, before the salad goes in. This saves on washing up but, more importantly, it gives you plenty of space to whisk the ingredients , meaning that they will emulsify and blend together properly. This doesn't happen very well if you shove everything into a glass jam jar and give it a shake, for example. The type of dressing to make depends on the salad leaves you are using. If you want a more robust dressing, you might use more mustard and a well-rounded vinegar, like red wine vinegar. For a sharper, tangier taste, try white wine vinegar, and for something softer use a cider vinegar. Walnut oil can replace olive oil and is delicious with sherry vinegar over a salad of baby spinach leaves and very hot strips of bacon. A finely sliced shallot or spring onion or a few chives left in the dressing to soften (both in flavour and texture) for ten minutes can be very good, and so can a crushed clove of garlic. And so, of course, can various herbs (think of a mint vinaigrette over peas). But the dressing I make most often is a simple vinaigrette using four parts oil to one part vinegar, half a part mustard, salt and pepper.

For a large bowl of leaves (and never overdress a salad) put into the salad bowl half a teaspoon of **Dijon mustard** (I prefer it smooth for this purpose) and one dessertspoon of

white wine vinegar. Add a little **Maldon salt** and **black pepper** and whisk it all together, so that the salt dissolves into the vinegar. I either use a small magic whisk (the ones that look like they have a coil of wire wound around a loop on the end of a handle) or a clove of peeled **garlic** stuck into a fork – which, of course, adds a smidgen of garlic flavour into the dressing. Now add four desertspoons of your best **extra virgin olive oil**. Whisk all the time (a figure-of-eight movement is best) as you add the oil, one spoonful at a time, though you don't have to add it drip by drip by any means. By the time the last spoonful of oil has been whisked in you should have what looks like a pale yellow, slightly viscous, all-of-a piece vinaigrette. Now taste it. If it's too sharp, add more olive oil. Let it sit for a few minutes and taste it again to see if it needs more salt. Before you add the salad leaves, give it another quick whisk. It may not look like you have enough dressing, but you almost certainly will, as long as you toss the salad very well.

My mum, who doesn't make dressing or wash salad leaves, is nevertheless adamant about this last point. 'Toss it thirty-seven times, please,' she'll say to whomever she designates the task, and she is perfectly serious.

Such instructions are, of course, easy to follow, but implicit in them is a series of lessons that, once learnt, mean you can not only run up a couple of nice, juicy chops and a good salad, but that you understand larger principles: how oil and vinegar emulsify and therefore how other sauces will do the same. And about meat: where certain bits come from and how temperature control is important. The reason that the grill has to be so hot is because you want to create a seal – an envelope more or less – so that the chops' flavours and juices remain inside it. Meat contains albumen, which hardens when heated and, as in this case, you want it to harden very quickly in order to seal everything inside, so you have to expose the chops to a very high temperature.

The same principle applies whether you are cooking a steak or something larger, like, say, a fillet of beef....

Pops' party

The first time I cooked a fillet of beef was when my father – Pops – turned seventy-five, and my sisters and I threw him a lunch party in London for the old friends he sees too little of lately because, as he is not in the greatest health, he rarely leaves Somerset.

The party was to be in Rose and her husband Tom's bedroom, it being the emptiest room in their house and quite large. They dragged their bed and furniture into other parts of the house and asked a friend to paint a mural of a train across the walls. (Pops loves trains and has written a book about them: *Steel Wheels* by A.F Garnett. It's great! It opens by telling you, very succinctly, how the wheel was invented.) It is safe to say that they went to quite a lot of effort. I was to be in charge of the food – a self-appointed role. I would be going to quite a lot of effort, too.

When we asked Pops what he'd like to eat at his late-September party it was high summer and we'd spent July and August in Somerset eating courgette blossoms cooked in beer batter, tiny whole roasted beetroots and huge bowls of broad beans and fresh peas cooked with prosciutto and pearl onions.

'I don't know,' said Pops vaguely. 'Those yellow flowers? Some sort of big salad?'

But we couldn't make a salad for Pops' birthday lunch, not when we could no longer pick broad beans from the garden, and not in a room with a specially commissioned mural. Not with an octogenarian Russian poet among the twenty-five guests, my dad's godson Tom driving up from Wales, and my godfather Ben and his wife Yannick flying over from Mallorca for the occasion. We decided, along with platters of vegetables and bowls of couscous, to buy a long fillet of very good beef, sear it, and serve it with fresh horseradish. Rose hired a cheery Australian to help us hand out drinks and clear plates, so that we wouldn't be up and down from the table once the party started, especially as the dining table was a floor above the kitchen. He (as he told us as soon as he arrived) was not really a waiter at all but a trained chef. He made this even clearer as he watched me cook.

I'd really never cooked a fillet of beef before Pops' birthday lunch. But I'd eaten it and read about cooking it,

and not long before had watched a friend who is a chef (Mark Hix) cook one for a great many people. It seemed simple enough. I rang Mark for exact instructions. He was very clear and told me to sear it all over in a very hot pan on the top of the stove, and then put it in a very hot oven for fifteen minutes only, then take it out, wrap it in foil, and let it rest for another fifteen minutes, longer if we had the time. Naturally enough, that's what I planned to do.

'Fifteen minutes?' asked the Aussie. He made no secret that he felt far more qualified to cook the meat than me, and I, still a nervous cook at this stage, tended to agree with him.

'No way will a slab of meat that size be cooked in fifteen minutes,' he said, and laughed.

'We want it rare,' I said.

'Yeah,' said the Aussie. 'Course you do. But fifteen minutes!' He laughed again. He seemed to find it the merriest thing. I wasn't all that confident to begin with; it was an £80 piece of meat. Fifteen minutes, when it was up, did seem very little time. We cut into the meat and peered inside. It was frighteningly pink.

'No way!' the Aussie said, reeling back in horror. 'That's not pink. That's raw.' We put the fillet back in the oven. Then, after a few minutes, we repeated the ritual. In case that wasn't excruciating enough, we repeated the ritual again.

By the time the meat came out of the oven for the third time, had rested and was carved, it was overcooked. I was so upset I wanted to poke my eyes out. Now – three years and many seared fillets of beef later – I am over it, but only just. Of course the party was great, and nobody really cared about the beef except me, but I *really* cared. I almost cried. Still, I learnt three lessons:

1 Don't try something new when you are cooking for a lot of people.
2 Trust your instincts. If someone thinks you should add more salt or lemon or garlic, or cook a fillet of beef for longer, but you are not sure you agree with them, stick to your guns; you're the cook, not them. Let them fuck up in their own kitchens.
3 Let it go. When I think about how bothered I was by a piece of overcooked meat, I worry that I need help.

How to cook a fillet of beef

The fillet comes from the bit of the cow underneath the sirloin, which means it's been protected from having to do any work. Although it's by no means the most flavourful cut of beef (and some chefs eschew it for this reason), it is the most tender. And sometimes, especially when you have fresh horseradish to hand, tender hits the button. The worst part of a fillet of beef is how much it costs. There's no way round the expense, except to say that the pay-off is almost certainly worth it. It's a luxury, and cooking and eating it is definitely luxurious. I make it most often when there are just two of us for supper, along with fresh horseradish, purple sprouting broccoli, green salad and sourdough bread – a meal fit for a king.

Once you've got the timing right for this kind of meat (and by that I mean any cut that must be cooked quickly and is sensitive to heat), the rest is simple. Think of it as a pale beauty in the sun without sunscreen – keep watch! Have a care! There's no reason why, unlike me, you shouldn't get it spot on first time.

First, prepare the meat

Make sure that the fillet is in one fairly evenly shaped long log. Trim the fat from the fillet and take off any lingering membrane (or ask your butcher to do this for you). It's easy to buy the right amount because the butcher can show you with his knife how much you might slice off for each person you are serving. A fillet weighing around 800g will feed four to six people, depending how greedy everyone is. I never buy less than 400g, even for just two of us. Sometimes you'll buy the fillet and it will have an extra chain of beef attached, like a sort of flappy bat's wing. Trim this off (it's easier to get the timing right if you are dealing with one uniformly sized piece) and put it in the fridge or freezer for another day's treat.

Now, marinate

A fillet will benefit from marinating overnight (or, even better, for up to 24 hours), but it's worth doing even for just an hour if you're short on time.

The marinade can be as simple as a slick of olive oil and some freshly ground black pepper, but I usually push the boat out a bit further and gather some **thyme** leaves, **parsley** stalks and leaves, **black peppercorns** (about a tablespoon of each), the zest of half a **lemon** or so, a clove of **garlic** and a good slosh of **olive oil** (about 100ml), and I crush it all together in a pestle and mortar, so it becomes a paste.

Pour and scrape the marinade paste into a freezer bag large enough to hold the fillet. Add the fillet to the bag and, using your hands, rub the marinade into it so that the meat is well covered. You can do this in a bowl, but a bag means that the meat is surrounded on all sides by the marinade. Seal the bag tightly and put it into the fridge for a whole day, overnight or a few hours. (If you are marinating for just one hour, don't bother putting it in the fridge.) Take it out of the fridge at least half an hour before cooking, so that it reaches room temperature.

And then, cook it

Make sure that the marinated meat is at room temperature. Heat the oven to 220°C/425°F/gas mark 7. Take the meat out of the marinade and keep the marinade to one side in the freezer bag.

Heat two tablespoons of **groundnut oil** or sunflower oil in a roasting tin on the hob until it is really hot. Carefully place the fillet into the hot pan. It absolutely should sizzle. Loudly. Let it sizzle and sear on one side before turning it over, using sturdy, long-handled tongs. Make sure each side is properly seared – that it is brown and beginning to caramelise all over. This will take about six to eight minutes in all.

Put the beef still in its roasting tin into the hot oven for fifteen minutes only. Ten or twelve minutes means it will be even pinker, which to my mind is even better. Once the fifteen minutes are up, whip it out of the oven and put it on a serving board or plate and cover it loosely in aluminium foil, so that it keeps warm and rests – it will continue cooking while it rests, which is why it needs so little time in the oven.

While this is happening make a sauce. Everyone loves it.

Strain the reserved marinade from its freezer bag and pour into the pan, along with about 150ml or a couple of ladle's-worth (it depends, of course, on how many you are feeding) of **good beef stock** if you've got it, chicken if not, and a good slosh of red wine. Let all this bubble up and whisk it together so that it deglazes the pan and incorporates any bits of meat or marinade stuck to the bottom of the tin. When it is bubbling away and has reduced somewhat, whisk in a good slice of **butter**, in chunks. You can add more than one chunk at a time, but use your whisk. The point is for the butter and the sauce to emulsify – otherwise you'll end up with a thin brown gravy with butter floating on top. If this happens then you are better off skimming the sauce and serving it as juice. But if you whisk and heat and watch your sauce carefully then it will all come together. I add as much butter as I dare, probably about 20g.

Sometimes, because this last step happens shortly before eating, a guest will be watching over Cook during these final crucial minutes, often giving off disapproving vibrations re: the butter. This kind of audience is to be discouraged. The butter gives the sauce its silkiness, as well as making it tasty and properly satisfying. Disapproving diners are welcome to abstain.

Horseradish

It is getting easier and easier to buy horseradish in good greengrocers, which is a relief because it is one of those things that lifts any meal involving beef or smoked fish. I used to have to order it a day or two before I wanted to buy it, but my local butcher now stocks it all-year-round. What you don't need, you can freeze and, when you come to use it again, grate it straight from frozen (if you let it defrost first it winds up a bit limp and soggy). It is important to grate horseradish, once it is peeled, across the grain, otherwise you will end up with a pile of long fibres. And use a fine grater – a microplane is best because it is so sharp.

I sometimes make a horseradish cream using crème fraîche and red wine vinegar (that recipe accompanies the beef, horseradish and celeriac stew in Chapter four). Recently, however, Rory O'Connell gave me a recipe for a horseradish cream. Rory, is a chef and teacher, who co-founded the Ballymaloe Cookery School in East Cork, Ireland, with his sister Darina Allen. He still teaches there, as well as running private classes from his own beautiful house nearby in Ballycotton. (Rory is a friend as well as my sometime teacher, and I met him through another fantastic

Irish chef, Canice Sharkey, who runs the restaurant Isaac's in Cork and lives in the house I would most like to own in the world. Canice I met through Gordon the antique dealer. See how it all joins up?)

There have been several cooks integral to either my learning to love cooking or my actual learning to cook, including my friend, Nell, in New York, Rose Gray on holiday in Shelter Island, and Rory in Ireland.

Horseradish cream

Here is how Rory taught me to make horseradish cream. Even a short recipe like this is accompanied by important lessons, which add to one's store of understanding and knowledge. I use this recipe when I have more time and want something more layered and subtle and velvety than horseradish with crème fraîche and vinegar. A fillet of beef sings out for it.

The secret is to use fresh horseradish and follow the recipe to the letter. Be utterly accurate.

Finely grate three tablespoons of **horseradish** across the grain. In a bowl whip 225ml of **cream** softly.

(Never over-whip cream, whatever you are using it for: its not very agreeable when it gets stiff and buttery, and though at the beginning of whipping cream, whether by hand or using an electric whisk, it seems to take an age for anything to happen, it can turn quite quickly.) Whip it until it still collapses in on itself in gentle folds, and then STOP. Don't be tempted to give it a few more goes for good measure.

Once it is whipped, mix the cream and horseradish together with one teaspoon of granulated **sugar** (this small amount will not sweeten the cream, but simply lifts the taste of the horseradish), a quarter of a teaspoon of **mustard powder**, one teaspoon of **white wine vinegar**, one teaspoon of **lemon juice**, plus **salt** and freshly ground **black pepper**, to taste. Do not over-mix everything or it may curdle; the elements need bringing together rather than beating about.

Once mixed together, chill it in the fridge. This will allow the flavours to merge together properly and it is important that the cream is served stone cold, which works particularly well with hot food.

Chapter two
How I came to cooking.
**Roasting my first
chicken on a sailboat
in the middle of the
Atlantic, and other
lessons**

My first roast chicken

The first time I roasted a chicken was in a small oven that swung on its hinges in the narrow galley kitchen of a sailboat, somewhere off the coast of Florida. It was the first night of a journey across the Atlantic Ocean from America to Portugal and, because I had never sailed before, it was assumed by my four male companions that I would be the chef. I didn't tell them that I had actually never cooked before either.

'Have you made a shopping list?' Michael, the skipper, asked me over dinner at a Florida crab shack a week before we set sail. The men were spending their time drilling holes to make sure our lifeboat was secure, and doing many other important tasks. I was happy to scrub the deck, sandpaper window frames and run errands, but make a list? No, I hadn't made a list. I'd assumed we'd all make a list together, or better still, they'd make a list and I'd nod in agreement. What do you buy for a month or two at sea to feed four people three times a day?

'A list?' I replied. 'Yes. Sort of. A sort of list.'

Michael looked mildly irritated. 'Very amusing,' he said. 'Remember you need to think about amounts. Remember everything has to be stored. Remember to get anchovies and salted almonds. Remember two of us will be working nightshifts every night, so we'll need things to keep us awake through that. And remember to get a chook so you can roast it on the first night.'

I hated the idea of cooking. I believed myself to be a born sous-chef, a contented beta: happy to be in the kitchen, thrilled to help, first to wash up. But to take responsibility for turning out a meal? I once watched an artist friend (a man who cultivated a sort of feyness) trying to turn over a fish that he had been co-opted by his wife to barbecue.

'Oh God,' he said as the fish

collapsed in his tongs and fell into the embers of the fire. 'Typical,' he snapped. 'This is why I should never be put in charge of the barbecue. A) I can't do it, and B) I hate it.'

That's exactly how I felt as I stared at the raw chicken on our first night at sea. It had string wound round it. Was I supposed to put it in the oven in its bondage or should it be released? Lighting the oven seemed to require me to turn on the gas, put my head very far inside, and waggle a lit match around. It wouldn't light. A) I couldn't do it, and B) I hated it.

I tried so hard and for so long to light the oven that the kitchen began to fog up with panic. A storm had just ended, the men were getting hungry, we didn't want to eat in the dark, and if I asked for help so long after descending to the kitchen to start supper then the men would know my failure and I didn't think they'd laugh. I cried. Then I called up to the deck.

'Dave?' Dave was, in effect, Michael's first mate on our journey, as well as his brother-in-law. He is an endlessly patient, sweet-natured man, who looks like a 1930s' schoolboy and consistently finds the fun in

anything: a lightening storm, say, or a broken loo. An unlit oven, I hoped.

'Dave? The oven? Am I? Is it? I think...perhaps? Would you...?' Dave did. Three times over three nights he had to light the oven for me (and we did begin to laugh) before I mastered it on my own, but, in fact, that first befuddlement over the oven, with its tears of frustration and panic, was the worst thing that happened to me as a first time cook sailing across the Atlantic Ocean over two months.

All you do to cook, after all, is cook. It's not trigonometry. There is nothing secret about it. If you can turn the oven on and get the chicken in, it will cook. If it's not done, you put it back in for longer. The rest is a question of degree: how tender do you want your chicken? How tasty? What do you want to eat it with? How do you want those things cooked? Or a question of ambition: how delicious can you make it? What best to accompany it? How to follow it?

I'd seen other people put a chicken in the oven and it come out an hour or so later brown and glistening. I knew it needed some butter or oil somewhere, and I knew it couldn't be pink when it came time to eat it. It was Michael who came down the galley stairs just as I was about to put the bird into the at-last hot oven.

'Oh,' he said, looking at the chicken. 'You roast it breast-side down first, do you?' Did I? I hadn't noticed. It seemed I did.

That's how I roasted my first chicken – blindly. I also peeled some potatoes and put them in the oven with the chicken about half way through. That's how I learnt that potatoes take at least as long as a medium sized chicken to roast properly. Apparently I was 'resting' the chicken as we waited for the spuds to cook. I asked Dave to carve and he pretended not to notice the slashed carcass (I'd stabbed and poked it all over to check it was cooked). Then, because the meat looked dry, I poured the juices from the pan over each plate.

We were all pleased to eat. We'd set sail hours before and had already watched a lightening storm on the horizon, then sailed through it, changed into foul weather gear, hoisted in sails, been shouted at, and proved a clumsy crew. Finally, sitting down to dinner, we were dry, we were drinking beer and the sea was calmer. We were very hungry and very tired. The food could only have been good. Except it wasn't really.

'Mmm,' said Michael, as he ate. 'Dave carve, did he?' He chewed his meat for a bit longer and raised his eyebrows. 'Next time, we might encourage him to spoon the fat from the gravy before chucking it over the chicken, so that our supper is not spoiled by congealed fat.'

Roast chicken

Now, if I were waving off my younger self in Fort Lauderdale, Florida, I'd say:

'Buy thyme; buy tarragon. The lemons you've bought aren't just for slicing up in a gin and tonic. Buy the best chicken you can find. Wash it inside and out and pat it dry, then season and flavour the inside cavity – with a lemon cut in two and a bunch of tarragon if you've got it, or use thyme or half an onion or a few cloves of garlic (flattened slightly with the edge of the knife), or a combination of those things, depending on what you have handy and what else you are cooking and what the weather is like.'

In winter there isn't tarragon growing freely in a pot on your balcony, but the warm flavours of onion and garlic will hit the spot. In summer, you may want a fresher, lemonier flavour. Rub butter over the outside of the chicken. Some people melt it in a small saucepan and pour it over, rubbing it into the skin. Others push it, sometimes mixed with herbs, under the skin of the breast, as though it were padding. A lemon squeezed over the outside and rubbed in is good, too. And salt and pepper are essential.

Roast the chicken in a hot oven, breast-side down, so that it stays juicy, and turn it over half-way through its cooking time, which is about an hour and fifteen minutes for a large chicken. (Test it by sticking your knife in its thigh – just the one place is enough – and if the juices run clear it's done; if they are pink, it's not.) About an hour into cooking, pour some **white wine** into the bottom of the tin, so that the chicken steams a little bit and you have more liquid for gravy. (But, if you don't have any wine or you forget this step, it doesn't matter.)

When the chicken is done, take it out of the oven and let it sit on a plate or board with a bit of foil over it to keep it warm, resting, so that the meat relaxes and the juices run back through the flesh. This is when you make the gravy, which you do by first spooning the fat from the top of the juices in the bottom of the pan. (If you happen to have a gravy-separating jug, then so much the better, if not, use a spoon, which is a bit of a pain in the arse, but worth it.) Use some kitchen paper to soak up the last bit of fat, though it doesn't matter if you don't get absolutely all of it – some fat is tasty; too much is greasy. Scrape up any bits of chicken or juice stuck to the bottom of the pan and add some water or more wine or a little **stock**, depending on what you've got, and let it sizzle on top of the stove. The longer you leave it to sizzle, the thicker it will get, but don't let it reduce too much or it will disappear.

Before we'd set sail I'd thought to myself: maybe I won't have to actually cook. If I make sandwiches for lunch every day and do the breakfast and always wash up and help chop, then the actual cooking of the actual supper might fall to someone else. But, after our first night at sea (a long night for Michael and Dave who'd taken the first night shift), it dawned on me that I'd be the only member of our crew keeping regular hours. Toby (a set designer from Los Angeles) and Jeremy (a windsurfing vegan) would alternate the night shifts with Michael and Dave, and the four of them would grab sleep whenever they could.

Meals, I also realised, were crucial. They would often be the only time all five of us would be together. They would provide us with natural breaks throughout the long hours of the day, and would be something to look forward to, signalling a shift in gear, a livening up, a gathering of energy – or a release of it, depending on what else was happening. I realised that we were sailing across a very wide ocean and, on the whole, our role was a reactive one.

So, I had a choice: I could either sit on my arse and behave like a piece of old baggage, or I was going to have to step up to the mark and learn to light the oven by myself.

I learnt quickly. On day two, for example, Michael wanted anchovies on toast for his breakfast.

'What is this?' he asked, when I sent up a piece of toast that I had spread thickly with a tin of anchovies, as though they were marmalade. He laughed incredulously. The plate came back down the stairs smartly.

'I can't eat this. One anchovy, Daise,' Michael said. 'If that. Half an anchovy. The merest whiff of anchovy. Open the tin in the next-door room and wave the toast around so it catches just the scent of anchovy. And what are you doing down in the kitchen sending food up here? No one is the maid on this boat. There'll be none of that nonsense. We eat at the same time, together.'

So, that's how I learnt:

1 To spoon the fat off the juices at the bottom of the roast-chicken pan before 'chucking it over the chicken'. (Advanced gravy skills would come a little later on.)

2 To be sparing when using anchovies, yes, but, in more general terms, to think about how ingredients work together. If I'd bothered to taste, or even open my nose enough to smell, what I was spreading so lavishly onto Michael's toast I would have put the brakes on. Anchovies are strong; toast is mild. These things aren't combined randomly, they need to be balanced.

3 That cooking is not the job of a martyr. I might have been the cook on the boat, but I was not the general maid. Eating food that someone has cooked for you is only enjoyable if that someone has enjoyed the process of cooking it.

But still, it took quite a while longer for the penny to drop, for the switch to flick, the one that transformed cooking from being a tiresome chore that I just had to do, to being a magical, alchemical and inspiring pleasure.

On the boat

day one

As soon as we left Fort Lauderdale we passed our first storm, which we sat and watched like a movie. That is, until it hit us and we got very wet.

Lunch Goats' cheese, avocado and tomato sandwiches on slices of fresh sourdough bread, followed by grapes. There was some drama halfway through the meal when I tipped over the sandwich plate on deck before the skipper had had even a bite to eat. I managed to scrape something off the floor for him.

Dinner Roast chicken and rosemary roast potatoes with a fresh, green salad. Dave helped. I fumbled around the tiny kitchen and cried. Not a great start.

After we'd finished dinner we caught a small, but perfectly formed, tuna, which Jeremy (a dreadlocked vegan), killed, by biting its head not *quite* off, but almost. Michael did the honours by cutting it up for us on deck, and we ate it raw with wasabi and soy sauce, which, miraculously, we have in our stores. This means that I have done something right. It melted in the mouth like butter.

day two

No land in sight.

'A long hot day,' said Michael. It was.

Breakfast Toast with (seemingly too many) anchovies for some, and marmalade for others. I also made oatmeal, as requested, which took an insufferably long time to cook. I think we might have bought the wrong kind.

Lunch BLTs.

Dinner Pasta and courgettes with Parmesan and fresh basil leaves from the plant we bought, which hopefully will continue to grow. Michael says that the next time we do a trip like this we should plant a whole herb garden on the boat. Where, pray? And anyway, next time? But the pasta seemed to be a success, and, more importantly, I didn't have to try to light the oven.

21:53 UFO sighting.

Other sightings A whole fleet of dolphins; a white tailed tropicbird; various cruise ships.

Pasta with courgettes

I knew how to boil pasta before I got on the boat. (And, by the way, 100g is about the right amount of pasta to cook per person.) On the boat, we used sea water to boil it in. We also washed up in sea water, and showered in it, too, using the American washing up liquid *Joy*, which lathers up well, even in cold salt water, for our hair and bodies as well as for the plates and pots and pans.

So, what did I do with the courgettes? I chopped them into thin discs and fried them up with some garlic and chilli, although I might not have bothered with the garlic and chilli on the boat – we would have compensated with lots of Parmesan, salt and pepper.

It's a useful thing to be able to do, pasta with courgettes, because courgettes are one of those vegetables that seem to breed in the bottom of the fridge. Certainly, in Somerset, I am always amazed at the quantities of courgettes we always have.

Here are two recipes for using courgettes with pasta (the latter is from the *River Café Two Easy* book. I swear, every recipe in that book is worth cooking):

Pasta with courgettes: a basic but delicious dish

This is one of those recipes that cooks call a 'store-cupboard recipe', which is frankly off-putting. It makes it sound like a loser, last resort sort of a recipe, like the dregs of a bottle of wine. This isn't like that at all, but it's still handy for when all you seem to have are courgettes, which you can also buy pretty easily without having to go to a butcher or fishmonger or deli.

Serves 4

As you prepare the **courgettes**, cook the **pasta** (any kind) in a large pan of boiling salted water, according to the packet instructions.

Wash about 800g to one kilo of **courgettes**. I peel off strips off their skin with a vegetable peeler, so that they look stripy. If they are very young and small and their skin is nice and thin, then, of course, you don't need to do this, but if they are a bit old and their skin is starting to get a little coarse, this is a brilliant way of 'jzooshing' them up. Top and tail them and then cut them into fine discs, like 2p coins.

Heat some good **olive oil** in a wide sauté or frying pan. The size of the pan is really the only trick to cooking courgettes well – they need to cook in a single layer, more or less. If you pile them high in a too-small saucepan, they'll steam in the juices that they release, which means they'll end up soggy and lifeless.

Add some chopped **garlic** (I use about two cloves, but, again, it depends on the time of year and the strength of the garlic) and/or a finely sliced **red chilli** (I always seed them, but that's up to you – it depends how hot you like your food as the heat is mostly in the seeds). Cook gently, stirring, until the garlic is golden brown – but be careful not to let it burn. The olive oil will become wonderfully flavoured by the garlic and chilli.

Throw in the courgettes, keeping them roughly in a single layer – you may need to cook them in batches. Let them brown a little and stir them around so that they cook on both sides. Some will brown more quickly than others, but having the variation works well.

Season with **Maldon salt** and freshly ground **black pepper**. At this point I also like to add in a whole load of chopped **parsley** leaves, and some torn **basil** and fresh **marjoram** if I have any. Add a good squeeze of **lemon juice**, too.

Drain the pasta when it is *al dente* (reserving a tablespoon of the cooking water). Add the pasta with the reserved cooking water to the courgettes and mix everything together well. Grate plenty of fresh **Parmesan** over the top and serve at once.

Spaghetti with squid and courgette
from *River Café Two Easy*
by Rose Gray and Ruth Rogers

Serves 4

500g squid
400g courgettes
400g spaghetti
3 tbsp good olive oil
dried red chilli, crumbled

2 garlic cloves, peeled,
  finely sliced
juice and zest 1 lemon
2 tbsp marjoram

1 Finely slice the squid from the body and separate the tentacles so that they are in tiny bite-sized pieces. (Make sure that the fishmonger prepares the squid for you by scraping off its pulpy membrane and squeezing out the beak etc. This is pretty standard practice when buying fresh squid, and squid must always be very, very fresh. Don't buy it unless you are going to use it later the same day.)

2 Wash the courgettes and grate them at an angle on the large side of a grater. Sprinkle with a salt and drain in a colander for fifteen minutes.

3 Start cooking the spaghetti in a large pan of boiling salted water, according to packet instructions.

4 Wash the salt from the courgettes and pat dry. This will get rid of some of the moisture that they carry around with them.

5 Heat a large heavy-bottomed frying pan over a medium heat, add the oil and when it is smoking hot add the squid. Stir briefly, then season with Maldon salt, freshly ground black pepper and the chilli. Add the courgettes and garlic. Stir-fry to just brown the squid and soften the courgettes. Add the lemon juice and zest and the marjoram and stir well. Remove from the heat.

7 Drain the spaghetti when it is *al dente* and add to the squid mixture. Toss together and serve at once.

42

day three

One-hundred and thirty-seven miles covered since yesterday. Some problems with the spinnaker sail, but we have a good wind and so we are happy. Boiling hot.

Breakfast Fruit salad, which was more successful than the anchovies.

Lunch Sandwiches with avocado, watercress, goats' cheese and gently fried courgette slices.

Dinner Roast chicken (the second one, before it goes off) with roast potatoes and broccoli and half a bottle of red wine. I lit the oven myself, but it kept switching off, or at least that's what I thought because the blue flames were always out when I went to put the chicken in. After several re-lighting sessions, I called Dave. He explained that that is what happens when it gets hot – the blue flames go out; the oven stays hot. Oh.

Tonight, at dinner, Jeremy asked, 'Where did you learn to cook?' I mumbled something about Shelter Island and watching Nell and Michael and Sarah. I didn't tell him that he was eating the second chicken I'd ever roasted – the first being two nights ago.

20:30 Disaster with the spinnaker, which wound itself round the mast like an umbrella.

'That's the worst wind I've ever seen,' Michael said gloomily when he came into the cockpit.

Sightings A plastic bottle; a smallish piece of wood; a large plank; a shooting star – I wished for my own E. C., a man I left behind in NYC and who I would never have been mine, properly, anyway.

day four

One-hundred and twenty miles since yesterday.

5:30–8:30 The boys fought with the spinnaker to unwrap it from the mast. At one point three of them nearly fell overboard.

Breakfast 'Lashings of toast and marmalade', to recover. And jam. Tea and coffee, like in a hotel, and mango juice from the tin. The reality of what we are doing occasionally registers: I cannot get off this boat. I cannot go back. I cannot change my mind. This is day four. There will be day five, six and seven….

Lunch Alessi (posh packet) soup with added olive oil and Parmesan, and ham sandwiches. I am in a bad mood and feel both un-useful and like a maid – a bad combo. Who wants to boil water and open packets of soup? **Dinner** Michael's broccoli pasta, cooked by Michael. It was delicious. Plus radicchio and celery salad. I've always hated celery, now I'm making salads out of it. What next? A near disaster with the carrots – they are fermenting in their plastic bags and infecting all our veggies. I washed everything and threw out the crap.

No boats. No fish. Where are all our fish?!

Michael's broccoli pasta

Michael makes this a lot, not just on the boat, and it is delicious. When I made it for Pops once I was home his heart sank visibly.

'I'm not mad about broccoli,' he said, 'I feel as if I'm eating a tree.'

But then he had this pasta and loved it. The broccoli has to be cut up small enough so that each bit of it absorbs the oil flavoured with chillies, anchovies and garlic. Orecchiette (the shells) is the best pasta to use because the bits of broccoli get lodged inside the shells, so every mouthful is flavourful, but I usually use penne, and so does Michael, which is good too, as that, along with spaghetti, is what I always have in the cupboard.

Serves 4

Cut about 800g **broccoli** into small pieces. Purple sprouting broccoli is the best broccoli – and one of the best vegetables – in the world, so if it's in season and you can get it, use it. It's best to cut the broccoli vertically, more or less, so that you end up with mini florets, plus a few chunks from the top of the stems. If it's sprouting broccoli then use the leaves, too. Steam or blanch the broccoli briefly, either over or in boiling salted water (it doesn't matter which method you choose, although blanching is quicker). Drain thoroughly.

Heat a couple of tablespoons of good **olive oil** in a large sauté or frying pan and add two cloves of **garlic**, cut into slivers. Fry the garlic gently, until it turns a pale brown – don't let it burn. Add either a dried (crush it in your fingers first) or fresh **chilli** (seeded and finely diced). (Add more chilli if you like it hot, and the same goes for garlic – add more if you like it extra garlicky.)

Add four or five salted **anchovies**. Before using them, gently rinse the salt off under the tap and pull the fillet away from the bone. Let the anchovies melt in the pan. The oil will have become flavoured with the chilli, garlic and anchovy. Add the partly cooked broccoli and cook gently, stirring, so that it softens, until it is just on the verge of becoming mushy.

Meanwhile, cook the **pasta** in a large pot of boiling salted water according to the packet instructions. Drain the pasta when it is *al dente* (reserving a tablespoon of the cooking water). Add to the broccoli (with the reserved cooking water) and mix well. Season with **Maldon salt** (remember that anchovies are salty, so go easy) and freshly ground **black pepper**. Add lots of freshly grated **Parmesan** and serve, as with all pasta, immediately.

day five

I slept well for the first time and feel one-hundred per cent better for it. Everyone is happier.
Breakfast Grapefruit juice, coffee, tea and oatmeal.

There is a rainstorm from the gulf, and the wind is dicking us around.

Sightings White tailed tropicbird and his mate; two large tunas – one bit, but no catch.

I made a lemon pound cake after I found a battered recipe book in the ship's library. That made me feel better and more useful – that's the trick. I am getting the hang of our days now: it is better to spend more time in occupation *vis-à-vis* the boat and the crew rather than reading poetry and trying to write all day. This is now our world and servicing it is satisfying. To that end I peeled and washed what felt like 8000 carrots.
Lunch Cheese, cucumber and lettuce sandwiches.
Afternoon tea Lemon pound cake.
Dinner Couscous, roasted veggies, roasted carrots in lemon juice and cumin, and a carrot salad with toasted pine nuts and pumpkin seeds. All fine and good, actually.

Jeremy came below deck to be a galley slave, but he got seasick and had to go back on deck, though not before asking me:

'Did your boyfriends cook for you?' I wanted to say: 'Boyfriends? Cook? Darling, I never made it as far as breakfast.'

Lemon pound cake

Pound cake gets its name because it was originally made using equal weights (a pound, unsurprisingly) of each key ingredient. This is a slight variation on the traditional recipe and produces a richer, more buttery cake.

Makes about 12 slices

3 large eggs
3 tbsp milk
1 ½ tsp vanilla extract
   (the good stuff)
170g plain flour, sifted
170g of caster sugar
3 tbsp poppy seeds
   (optional)
1 tbsp lemon zest, grated
¾ tsp baking powder
¼ tsp salt
195g unsalted butter, softened

for the syrup
60ml fresh lemon juice,
   strained
6 tbsp caster sugar

for the lemon icing
3 tbsp double cream
220g icing sugar, sifted
zest and juice of one lemon

1 Have all your ingredients at room temperature and preheat your oven to 180°C/350°F/gas mark 4. Grease and sprinkle with flour a 22cm-long loaf tin, or line the bottom with parchment paper.

2 In a largish bowl, whisk together the eggs and milk with the vanilla extract. In another, larger bowl, whisk together the plain flour, caster sugar, poppy seeds (if you are using them), lemon zest, baking powder and salt.

3 Add half of the egg mixture to the flour mixture along with the butter and beat on a low speed in a mixer, if you've got one (on the boat, by hand, the speed was certainly low), until the dry ingredients are moistened. Increase the speed to high (or try to)

46

and beat for exactly one minute. Scrape the sides of the bowl and gradually add the remaining egg mixture in two parts, beating for twenty seconds after each addition.

4 Scraping around the inside of the bowl transfer the batter to the tin and spread out the mixture evenly. Bake until a skewer or toothpick inserted into the centre comes away clean – about sixty-five minutes.

5 Just before the cake is ready, make the syrup to drizzle over it. This is an essential component. Place the strained lemon juice and sugar in a small saucepan and heat gently, stirring, until the sugar dissolves.

6 As soon as the cake comes out of the oven place it (still in its pan) on a rack and poke it all over with a wooden skewer and brush with half the lemon syrup. Let it cool in the pan for ten minutes, then slide a slim knife around the cake to loosen it from the pan, and invert it onto a greased rack. Peel off the parchment paper lining if you used one. Poke the bottom of the cake as you did the top and brush on some more of the syrup. Invert again onto another greased rack and brush the remaining syrup over the sides of the cake. Let it cool, right-side up on the rack. The cake is best if wrapped and stored in an airtight container for 24 hours before serving, but as if....

The lemon icing
To dot the i's and cross the t's, I also paint on a thin lemon icing made by gently heating the double cream and beating it together with the icing sugar until the mixture is smooth. Add the lemon zest and juice and a pinch of salt and mix together until smooth. You can always add in a bit more icing sugar or lemon juice if you think the consistency needs thickening or thinning, but bear in mind that the icing tends to thicken anyway, once it is left to settle.

47

A good carrot salad

This is very simple. Grate as many **carrots** as you can face. Always try to buy carrots that still have their dirt on them, as this seals in their flavour and means they haven't been washed by heavily chlorinated water. (The same goes for potatoes.) Wash them and peel them only if they need peeling. There is no point in using baby carrots for this salad, as they are often less flavourful than their larger counterparts, too fiddly to grate and better eaten when left whole.

In a small, dry frying pan, toast a mixture of **pine nuts**, **pumpkin seeds** and **sunflower seeds**, tossing them frequently and watching them carefully. Don't let them burn. The pumpkin seeds will take a little longer to toast, so put those in first.

Place the grated carrots in a large bowl, sprinkle the hot seeds and pine nuts over the top, then dress the salad. For the dressing, you will need plenty of **Maldon salt** and freshly ground **black pepper** mixed with three parts very good **olive oil** to one part fresh **lemon juice**. Pour everything over the top and mix it all together thoroughly, to coat.

day six

A beautiful morning. It doesn't feel like Groundhog Day today. Lots of clouds to look at. A 6:30 salt-water shower, then Dave, Toby and I scrubbed the boat down. And then we had a swim. Dave declared it the best swim of his life. I agreed.

Breakfast Coffee, tea, grapefruit juice and lemon pound cake.

I learnt how to tie knots: 1) a cleave knot, 2) a running cleave, 3) a square knot, 4) The Prince of Knots: the bowling knot, and 5) a figure-of-eight knot. The lesson took hours.

Lunch Ham, cheese, mayo and mustard sandwiches. Carrot and celery sticks. Lemon pound cake.

Dinner Pasta with bacon and peas, fresh basil and Parmesan, with a radicchio and celery salad. Followed by a Hershey's almond and chocolate bar. Rum and tonics as usual and we opened a bottle of red Beaujolais.

A starry night. Four-hundred miles to Bermuda.

Pasta with peas and bacon or ham: the basic and the five star version

The version we had on the boat was very good, and is another handy stand-by because you only need garlic, frozen peas and bacon to cook it. A long time after the boat trip I learned how to make a more refined version of this dish by way of an unbelievably glamorous friend called Victoria Fernandez, a Columbian woman who has lived in Paris, Tuscany and Portugal, as well as Bogotá and London, where she is based. She is a seriously good cook, and it was she who showed Thomas how to 'marinate' fresh peas overnight. He then played with it (as you do) when we were together in Ireland last summer. My contribution was to plonk on some Parma ham at the end. It was amazing.

Pasta with peas and pancetta: a weeknight supper
Serves 4

Put a large pot of salted water on to boil, for the pasta. Something long and flat like **tagliatelli** is good here, so that the peas and diced pancetta don't fall through it. At the same time, boil another, smaller pot of salted water and cook about 200g **frozen peas** for two or three minutes, or until they are cooked. Drain them and either run them under the cold tap to stop them cooking further or, even better, put them in a prepared bowl of iced water.

Meanwhile, heat about three tablespoons of good **olive oil** in a heavy-bottomed saucepan and start to cook a finely diced **red onion**. (In summer I often dispense with the cooked onion and use finely chopped raw spring onions added at the end with the mint instead. If you do this just go straight to the pancetta-cooking stage.) Cook the onion for about fifteen minutes over a low heat – you want it to be really soft and melted, but not too coloured.

Add about 150g of diced **pancetta** and a peeled and finely chopped **garlic** clove. Cook slowly over a low heat for another ten minutes. Season with **salt**, **pepper** and half a **dried red chilli** and add a handful of freshly chopped **mint**. Give everything a stir and add in the peas and a tablespoon or so of the pasta cooking water.

When the pasta is *al dente*, drain it and add to the peas and pancetta. Mix together and serve with plenty of **Parmesan** and a drizzle of olive oil.

Victoria and Thomas's pasta with peas and prosciutto: the glitzy version
Serves 4

You need **fresh peas** (about 300g, once podded) for this and they should be just picked. Fresh peas don't last long because once they are picked their sugar starts turning into starch. That's why the ones you buy in packets from the supermarket can taste mealy. You also need to start this dish the night before eating it, which is when you pod the peas – make sure you keep the pods – and put them in a bowl with two or three peeled whole shiny cloves of summer **garlic**, a few large **basil** leaves and a glug of good **olive oil**.

The next day, make a light stock in a saucepan by pouring cold water over the empty pea pods, to just cover them, and add a few whole black **peppercorns** and a sprig or two of **parsley**. Bring to the boil and simmer for about half an hour.

Cook the peas (having discarded the garlic and basil) in a medium sized pan of boiling salted water for a couple of minutes, or until they are cooked. Drain and refresh the peas in a bowl of iced water.

In another saucepan, heat three tablespoons of good **olive oil** and gently sauté a clove of finely chopped **garlic** until it begins to turn golden.

Boil a large pan of salted water and add the pasta – again, something long and flat like **tagliatelli** will work best.

Add the peas to the garlic and oil along with a spoonful or two of the pea stock. Let the flavours mingle and the peas heat through gently. Season with **Maldon salt** and freshly ground **black pepper**.

With a handheld blender, blitz about a third of the peas with another tablespoon of the stock so that you get a bright green purée. It should still be coarse, so don't blend it for too long.

When the pasta is *al dente*, drain it and add it with the pea purée to the pan with the peas.

Add plenty of torn **basil**, some more **olive oil**, a spoonful of the stock, grated **Parmesan** and check the seasoning. Mix everything together.

Finally, drape over a few slices of torn **prosciutto** (about one or two per person, and don't tear into very small pieces – you can even keep some of the slices whole). Let it wilt as you bring the pasta to the table.

day seven

Hot and sunny. No concept of days or time. Is it Monday, Sunday or Tuesday? Is it the 9th? I know it is July.
Breakfast Poached eggs on toasted English muffins, coffee and tea, and pound cake, which keeps on going.

Toby wore his boxers and a woolly hat on deck and looked like Winslow Homer. Michael shaved. Jeremy farted in Toby's face. We are sailing along. Two-hundred and twenty miles to Bermuda.

Lunch Same again – ham, cheese, mayo and mustard sandwiches. Carrot and celery sticks. And then the wind began. 17 knots of wind; 7 knots of speed, then 8, then 9.

I made chocolate chip and banana cookies following instructions on the back of a chocolate wrapper, but they came out like scones.

19:00 Beers on deck to celebrate our speed.

Dinner Ratatouille made with peppers, aubergine, courgettes and olives. Served with rice. If you follow the instructions on the packet of rice to the letter, it works perfectly. We sprinkled Parmesan on top of the ratatouille to beef it up.

Sightings Three shooting stars. One of them was like a UFO with showers of light coming from it. It seemed to plunge straight into the earth.

Slept in a rocking boat, jammed up against the port side of my bunk.

day eight

Still our speed goes on.

Breakfast Coffee and fruit salad made with an apple, two oranges, a tin of pears and lemon and lime juice. Plus the last of the pound cake.

Read about Walter de la Mer's gentle and serene death. Marcel Proust died on this day, 10th July, in 1871.

16:00 First sight of Bermuda and the very next instant we caught a beautiful tuna.

20:30 Arrive in Bermuda. I can't tie any of the knots I learnt. We have sailed over 1000 miles. Land seems hateful. We anchor near huge cruise ships, see a party boat and decide it is all too unbearable and so, despite exhaustion and a big struggle with the anchor, we get the hell out and find a better spot.

day nine

Last night, we motored to a place called Captain Smokey's Marina, which turned out to be a perfect spot. The marina consists of one blue building with a single shower, a loo and a grass lawn with a table, benches, an outside tap and a barbecue. There are no other people or boats to be seen. Dave took apart and mended our broken loo all afternoon on the green lawn. My hips are covered in huge bruises. Michael has rechristened the hardware store nearby Tiffany's; three rolls of kitchen paper cost $16.25.

Dinner Grilled tuna by Toby on the barbie and his delicious coleslaw (made by cutting up two cabbages – one red and one white – some spring onions and a red pepper). He dressed it by plonking on whatever caught his eye in what I thought was a rather too cavalier fashion. What caught his eye were mayonnaise, Worcester and soy sauce. I watched in amazement. I thought dressing could only be a combination of oil and vinegar, salt and pepper, and maybe some mustard and maybe some lemon juice and maybe some fresh herbs.

Worcester sauce? Soy sauce? I waited for the sky to fall in. But it worked. Jeremy, not to be outdone, made a salad, too. His mung beans have sprouted and so he mixed them with raisins and copied Toby with his dressing, though not to be outdone he added oil to the mix as well. Michael saw his creation and said: 'Jeremy's made what? Oh, I see. He's made a Jeremy.' In fact, it was delicious. It is a pleasure not to be cooking for a night.

Two good things to do with fresh tuna

The tuna we ate on the boat and in Bermuda was exceptional because it was so fresh. It is unlikely that I will often, or indeed ever again, eat tuna moments after it has been caught, but it is worth making sure that you get it as fresh as possible. It should be bright red, rather than dull or discoloured, which is a sign that the blood has started to oxidise and that it has, therefore, been exposed to the air for some time.

1 Tuna steaks with a caper and coriander dressing

You need one **tuna steak** (about 225g) per person.

Rub some good **olive oil** into both sides of the tuna steaks and season both sides with **Maldon salt** and freshly ground **black pepper**.

Heat a griddle pan and when it is very, very hot (let it heat for about ten minutes) place the tuna steaks on it. Let them cook for thirty seconds to a minute on each side.

Remove from the griddle and place them onto warmed plates and pour over a dressing made from (for four people): two tablespoons roughly chopped fresh **coriander** and two tablespoons salted **capers** (rinsed and patted dry), the zest and juice of two **limes**, two tablespoons **white wine vinegar**, two cloves of finely chopped **garlic**, two finely chopped **shallots**, a dessertspoon of **grainy mustard** and four tablespoons of good **olive oil**. Season, to taste, with **Maldon salt** and freshly ground **black pepper**. This dressing is based on a recipe that I found in a magazine, and is delicious.

2 Sesame tuna salad

In this recipe you only need one 225g **tuna steak** to feed four.

In a small bowl mix together three tablespoons of **soy sauce** and a dash of **Tabasco**. Smear a teaspoon of this on one side of the **tuna steak**.

Spread a dessertspoon of **sesame seeds** on a plate and put the smeared side down on the sesame seeds, pressing well to coat. Smear the top side of the tuna with another teaspoon of the sauce and coat with sesame seeds as well. Cover and chill for half an hour or so.

Mix one and a half tablespoons of **groundnut oil** with one and a half teaspoons of **sherry vinegar** and half the remaining soy sauce and Tabasco.

Mix the rest of the soy sauce and Tabasco with a desertspoon of **sesame oil** and set aside.

Heat a large frying pan until it is very hot, and then swirl a tablespoon of **groundnut oil** around the pan. Sear the tuna steak for one minute on each side, then leave to cool and rest for up to an hour.

Toss as many baby **spinach leaves** as you will eat in a salad in the groundnut oil and vinegar dressing.

Cut the tuna steak into narrow slices and season lightly with **Maldon salt** and freshly ground **black pepper**. Serve the tuna slices on top of the dressed spinach leaves and drizzle with the soy sauce, Tabasco and sesame oil mixture.

day ten

Bermuda: laundry, emails. I emailed E.C. and told him about my bruises, then downloaded some baking recipes, so that I can make things to help the boys get through their night shifts.

Lunch Jeremy offered to make lunch, as he can only be in the kitchen when the boat isn't moving. He spread peanut butter on some dry saltine crackers and put a raisin on top of each one.

'Jeremy might win the prize for this lunch,' said Michael.

We caught a bus to Hamilton to go shopping for our stores. $600 later we left the supermarket, with, of course, two chickens, as well as fresh fruit and veg, butter and milk. Jeremy insisted on buying endless nuts, seeds, dried fruit and bok choy. Bok choy? Does he think I can run to Chinese?

Put the stores in the boat, filled it with fuel and water and then we were off with a big wind.

Dinner Alessi Soup and bruschetta *a la* Rose in Shelter Island. Halfway through the meal Jeremy said:

'Look over there. Here comes some weather.'

It was a big squall – heavy rain, big waves, boat reeling. The boys can only hold the boat rather than steer it. The squall began to turn major and I was sent down below deck for the first time on the trip. Forty knots of wind. Boat going at a 10.4 knots.

day eleven

Major rolling. Rain. Huge, lumpy sea.
Breakfast 'We have to eat very, very simply when it is like this,' Michael told me, and then sent me downstairs to make proper Irish oatmeal for everyone, which takes at least forty minutes to make, and still tastes uncooked.

We had freezing cold fresh water showers by standing in the rain in our bathers.

Lunch Coleslaw, with my imitation of Toby's dressing, only not as good. Too much Worcester sauce? Too much soy sauce? I couldn't tell. Also cheese and cucumber sandwiches. I felt seasick being down below because of the waves.

Dave's mended loo works like a charm. I have my period. The storm continues. We covered 175 miles in twelve hours today, but the Azores is 2000 miles away. I would feel better about this if I felt less seasick and didn't face the prospect of roasting a fucking chicken tonight.

Dinner Roast chicken, roast potatoes and green beans – all cooked by me in my foul weather gear, with the boat violently rocking and the oven swinging hard on its hinges.

'Who'd have thought you'd turn out to be a fabulous ship's cook,' said Michael. I think he was referring to my perseverance rather than my culinary skills.

A lovely sliver of new moon hangs in the sky.

day twelve

I'm worried about the new broccoli going off. The Bermuda fruit and veggies aren't nearly as long lasting as the ones from Whole Foods in Florida. Is that a good or a bad thing?

Beautiful, bright sunny day. Sea much flatter.

Breakfast Mango, banana and grapefruit salad. Boys all exhausted after two days of such hard sailing. The oranges are going off – but oranges are not the only fruit.

Dinner I have to get rid of the other chicken before it goes off. Made coq au vin, by vaguely looking at the instructions in the ship's only recipe book.

Coq au vin

Dave jointed the **chicken** for me, but you can ask your butcher to do this.

Season the chicken with **salt** and freshly ground **black pepper**, then heat some **olive oil** in a large heavy-bottomed casserole and brown the meat in batches (if you overcrowd the pan the chicken begins to cook rather than brown). Remove the meat from the casserole and place to one side. (Better still would be to brown the chicken in **hot bacon fat**, which you can make by rendering down 115g of thickly sliced and cubed **bacon** over a medium-high heat. Remove the bacon once the fat has melted from it and it has coloured nicely. Keep aside with the browned chicken).

In the same pan (with the chicken now removed), cook a chopped **onion** and two medium-sized chopped **carrots** for about ten minutes.

Add a handful of **flour** and cook for a few minutes, then pour in a lot of **red wine** (don't use anything you wouldn't drink), a little less **chicken stock** (made from a stock cube on the boat, because needs must on the ocean), a squeeze of **tomato purée**, a couple of **bay leaves**, the leaves from a sprig of fresh **thyme** and a small handful of **oregano** leaves, chopped. Bring to the boil, stirring. (If you're using dried herbs, use a teaspoon each of thyme and oregano.)

Then the chicken pieces can go back in (and the bacon, too, if you've used it) with a handful of peeled **potatoes**, which isn't part of traditional recipes, but works very well. After it has come to the boil again, turn the heat down to low and put the lid on. Simmer gently for about thirty-five minutes, until the chicken and potatoes are cooked.

Skim off the fat from the surface before serving, and season with **Maldon salt**, freshly ground **black pepper** and chopped **flat-leaf parsley**.

day thirteen

The boys scrubbed the deck while I made us all breakfast.

Breakfast Tea, coffee and fruit salad with lots of the oranges because they are going, going, gone. And an English muffin for everyone.

Michael found the BBC World Service on the radio for the first time. America wants to attack Iraq.

Lunch BLTs with avocado. Jeremy made a salad from pumpkin seeds and pine nuts and we ate his sprouted sunflower seeds.

'Luscious,' said Michael.

The boys did something to the pole of the staysail and the boat careened about. Water poured in through the windows. The drawers flew out of the cabinet.

Dinner Toby helped me make a pasta dinner. He saw that it is neither as easy nor as pleasant to boil a huge pot of water when the boat is rocking away and the sea is lumpy.

He sautéed lots of aubergine, which was going off, with garlic and red chilli flakes, while I made a bean salad using the green beans I'd topped and tailed and sliced vertically in three for hours. I mixed them with a tin of lima beans and some diced red onion and dressed it all in a thick mustardy vinaigrette. It was good.

Everything is damp. Two of the bunks are sodden.

day fourteen

Beautiful morning. Lots of wind. Huge waves. The boat is still careening about.

Breakfast Coffee, tea and toast with anchovies – my least favourite breakfast request.

We laid the wet mattresses out on deck to dry. I did a veg. inspection; we have to eat bok choy for lunch. My heart sinks at roasting vegetables, but it will have to be done. Every so often huge chunks of wave land on us in the cockpit. We get used to being soaked through. It feels like we are riding a bucking bull.

Lunch Cheese and ham sandwiches. It is hard to be down below deck in the kitchen when the is boat rocking so much.

Dinner Hours of roasting veg., one tray at a time, in the small oven. Toby cooked the bok choy, thank God. He sautéed it with ginger, celery and a little garlic.

During the night the wind turned into a gale. Winds up to 34 knots. I was frightened all night and thought we were going to drown.

day fifteen

And on it goes: grey waves like mountains; 34 knots of wind is now normal. It goes up to 41 knots, and whistles frequently. Everything is soaked through.

Breakfast Granola bars. It is too wavy to do anything else.

Lunch Plain cheese sarnies wrapped

in foil, so we could eat them while getting dunked on by the waves.
Dinner Alessi soup and toast.
Sighting White tailed tropicbird.

day sixteen

Nine-hundred and twenty-five miles on the clock and still the wind goes on, though a little less severely. I am dying for a shower. My hair is full of salt and grease and kitchen dirt.
Breakfast Tea, coffee and fruit salad. At least we have had something fresh and good. The mangoes from Bermuda are still succulent.
Lunch Sandwiches with avocado, tomato, slices of sautéed courgette and cucumber.

I have to bake something today to use up some of our butter, eggs and rotten bananas. I attempted a banana bread from a recipe I downloaded at the Internet café in Bermuda. It was not a great success, but it disappeared nonetheless.

Michael and I made bread using a recipe he got from Una, a cook he knows. (Five years later the very same Una would come to live with us in Somerset, though as a friend rather than a cook). It's a great recipe for the boat because it's made with lots of seeds and molasses, it doesn't need to rise, and it keeps for ages. Plus, it is very good humoured.

While we were making it, a huge wave entered through one of the hatches and dumped itself squarely into our nearly-done bread mix. Not a drop of water went anywhere else.

'Oh well,' said Michael. 'That'll be the salt then.'

I would have wept and thrown everything out of the same hatch, but Michael didn't even raise an eyebrow. And he was right; the bread was still delicious.

I showered by harnessing myself to the deck and letting the waves wash over me.
Dinner Ratatouille. It was a bit watery this time, I think because I used a can of chopped tomatoes instead of whole plum ones. Never mind. Also, carrot salad with sprouted mung beans.

I feel exhausted and damp and stiff.

We have passed the 1000-mile mark. The clocks went forward an hour. And we lost our fishing rod. The sea took it.

Una's brown bread

Makes two medium sized loaves

800g wholemeal flour
2 sachets of Easy blend fast
   action yeast
couple of good pinches
   (or one wave's worth) salt
2 dsp of molasses

2 dsp olive oil
butter, for greasing
seeds: a large handful of
   sunflower, pumpkin,
   sesame or cumin or a
   mixture of them all

1 Place the flour, yeast and salt in a bowl and mix together.

2 Dilute the molasses with 1.2 litres warm water. (The water should be blood temperature. If it is too hot it will kill the yeast; if it is too cold then the bread will take ages to rise.) Pour the liquid slowly into the flour mixture.

3 A spoonful at a time, add the olive oil and mix together. The mixture should be neither stiff nor sloppy, so add a bit more oil if you think it is too stiff.

4 Butter two loaf tins liberally, around the lips as well as the bottoms and sides to prevent the dough sticking.

5 Pour the mixture into the tins so that they are half full. Cover with a tea towel and leave for half an hour to rise. Towards the end of the rising time preheat the oven to 220°C/425°F/gas mark 7.

6 Place the tins in the oven and bake for forty minutes. Take the bread out of their tins for the last five to ten minutes, so that their bottoms are nice and crispy. When the bread is done it should sound hollow like a drum when tapped on the base.

day seventeen

At last: a beautiful sunny morning with endless clear skies.

Breakfast Michael/Una's bread, toasted, which was lovely, plus coffee and grapefruit juice.

I cut my foot on the edge of the coal fire in the saloon and the boys administered to it. Michael used a Kayapo Indian antiseptic, which he bought when he was filming in the Amazon about 100 years ago, and Dave used medic-wipes from his brother-in-law doctor's first class first aid kit.

Daily veg. inspection; threw out some celery. Thank God. Must cook the parsnips.

Sightings An upside-down desk bobbing along beside us; a British Storm Petrel, which flew around and around our boat.

I baked some gingerbread from one of the downloaded recipes and Michael and I made more Una bread. We added flax seeds to the mix, too, for a bit of extra texture. It is really very good bread indeed.

Lunch Cheese, cucumber and tomato sandwiches, and the remains of yesterday's carrot salad. Later in the afternoon we had a beer each with some roasted parsnip sticks, which everyone loved.

Dinner Toby cooked a frittata made with eggs, peppers, onions, potatoes, paprika and cumin. Plus we had Jeremy's mung bean sprouts and I made a salad of cucumber, celery, avocado and lima beans with a simple vinaigrette made from olive oil, a little vinegar, lemon juice and salt and plenty of ground black pepper.

Roasted parsnip sticks
Serves about 5 (depending on how greedy everyone is)

Preheat the oven to 200°C/400°F/gas mark 6. Peel five to seven **parsnips** and cut them in half lengthways, then in half again, so that you have long quarters. Carefully slice out the mealy central core of each quarter, so that you are left with a flat edge. Then cut them in half, lengthways, again. If the parsnips are too long, cut them in half, or even thirds, horizontally. (You want them to be about the same size as the carrot sticks that you might see in a child's lunch box.)

Rub them all over with plenty of **olive oil**, **Maldon salt** and freshly ground **black pepper**, then roast them in the oven until they are beginning to brown on the outside and feel a little soft when you squeeze them.

Remove from the oven and drain off any excess oil on some kitchen paper. Serve them with a beer and sprinkle with a little extra salt.

Note Some people like to add a little honey or crushed toasted cumin seeds to the parsnips just before they go into the oven, but I think the taste and texture of parsnips are sublime and should be left well alone.

Gingerbread

This is not quite the recipe that I used on the boat, which I still have. Instead it is one that was given to me by Rory O'Connell. He, in turn, was given it by Elizabeth Mosses, the mother of Irish artist Paul Mosses and potter Keith Mosses. Though the recipes aren't that different, I always use this one now, passed along from friend to friend, rather than downloaded from the Internet in Bermuda.

Makes two loaves, but it keeps well, wrapped up in foil in an airtight container and it freezes well, too

450g plain flour
½ tsp of salt
1 ½ tsp ground ginger
2 tsp baking powder
½ tsp bicarbonate of soda
 (baking soda)
handful of sultanas (optional)

225g soft dark muscovado
 sugar
170g unsalted butter, cut into
 cubes
340g treacle
300ml milk
1 free-range egg, lightly
 beaten

1 Preheat the oven to 180°C/350°F/gas mark 4. Line two loaf tins, approx. 23cm x 13cm each, with silicone or parchment paper.

2 Into a large, wide bowl, sieve together the flour, salt, ground ginger, baking powder and bicarbonate of soda. (It is worth measuring the bicarbonate of soda accurately and sieving it with your finest sieve before adding it to the other dry ingredients to make sure that there are no lumps in it. It is strong stuff.) The sieving is important to get some air into the mix.

3 Add the sultanas (you can leave these out if you don't like them, but they definitely add a big something to the finished cake).

4 In a saucepan over a low heat, gently warm the muscovado sugar with the cubes of butter and the treacle. Don't let the mixture get too hot; you should be able to put your finger in it.

5 Add the milk and stir together. Allow the mixture to cool a little.

6 Stir the wet mixture into the bowl of dry ingredients, and then stir in the egg.

7 Mix everything together thoroughly to ensure that there are no lumps of flour, but don't over beat or the cake will toughen up.

8 Divide the mixture between the prepared tins and bake for about an hour, or until a skewer or toothpick inserted into the loaves comes out clean.

9 Allow to cool in the tins, then remove and wrap in foil. Serve with butter and honey… if you wish.

day eighteen

A beautiful, sunny, calm-ish day. The boys ate half a loaf of gingerbread on night watch.

Breakfast Tea, coffee, toast.

Sighting Many, many dolphins, like puppies leaping around the boat. We sang to them. Dolphins all day, in fact. Dolphins, dolphins, dolphins.

Lunch BLTs and BLAs (bacon, lettuce and avocado) and fruit salad, made with the last mango, orange and banana plus a tin of pineapple and fresh lime juice. Plus, a finger of gingerbread each.

14:00 Sighting A sperm whale. Magnificent. We are a very happy boat.

Dinner Spaghetti with pesto from a jar and Parmesan and coleslaw. We will *never* run out of cabbage. Bermuda mints for pudding (disgusting aftertaste).

day nineteen

One-hundred and seventy-five miles until we reach the island of Flores in the Azores.

Breakfast Coffee, tea and English muffins with poached eggs.

Can I be bothered to make cookies today? Does anyone want cookies? Am I in a baking frenzy?

Lunch No more bread. Hooray! Rice with vegetable mush (the last courgette, grated, with roasted parsnips and onion, garlic and tinned lima beans). Also, coleslaw with toasted pumpkin seeds and pine nuts.

I did bake. I used a very precious Cadbury's chocolate Fruit and Nut bar for the cookies.

Sighting A big, rusty filing cabinet.

Dinner Pasta with peas, bacon and Parmesan with a salad made from the last of the cucumber and celery. Cookies and white wine for pudding.

Jackie's SoHo loft cookies

This is the cookie recipe that I wish I'd had on the boat. Mine didn't come out quite right on our sail: the bottoms would burn or the middles would be too soft, like a scone.

I ate the right ones – the perfect cookie – years later, at a dinner given by Jackie and Jay, a wonderful couple who live in a loft in New York's SoHo. We guests had eaten a delicious meal cooked by Jackie, and then had had cheese and then berries. We were full. We said we couldn't eat another bite. And then the cookies came out and we ate them all. When I asked Jackie how she made such perfect cookies – quite flat, with a crunch, but just gooey enough inside – she replied:

'Oh, I got the recipe from the back of the Toll House packet.'

Toll House make chocolate chips and sell them in packets, which have a label declaring that they are America's favourite.

American chocolate, however, tastes different to English chocolate, so it doesn't matter that you can't find Toll House chocolate chips very easily outside the USA.

Instead, I use high-quality chocolate chips from the Chocolate Society, or else I cut up a really good bar of milk chocolate and use that instead. (You could use dark, of course, but because you're not actually cooking with it, it doesn't have to have a very high cocoa content.) This is not quite the Toll House recipe; I've cut down on the sugar a little bit and increased the quantity butter.

Makes about two dozen cookies

Preheat the oven to 190°C/375°F/gas mark 5. Lightly grease two baking sheets with **butter**. Into a bowl, sift 150g **plain flour** with 1/2 teaspoon **bicarbonate of soda** (baking soda) and 1/2 teaspoon fine **salt**.

In another bowl beat 125g of soft **unsalted butter** with 70g **granulated golden sugar** and 50g **light brown muscovado sugar**, until it is pale and has a creamy consistency. It is best to do this in a mixer, as it's far easier and will be more even.

Beat in one **free-range egg**, then gradually sift in all your dry ingredients and mix everything together until it is just combined. Don't work it too hard.

Stir in 150g of **chocolate chips**.

Spoon heaped teaspoonfuls of the cookie mixture onto the baking sheets and bake for nine to eleven minutes, until they are pale golden and still slightly soft in the centre. Leave them for two minutes before removing them to a wire rack to cool. (You can keep this mixture in the fridge until you need it and make the cookies in smaller quantities.)

day twenty
8:45 sighting Flores.

All my cookies evaporated during night watch. Good.

Breakfast Coffee, tea and a fruit salad made from a tin of peaches and a banana.

Flores looks so beautiful. It is green and busy and covered in hydrangeas, like an Easter bonnet. Waterfalls tumble down the cliffs, there are crags and ravines everywhere and more flowers than you can believe.

We arrived at 6pm. There were twelve other boats in the port, including a very beaten up steel tub, sailed by one man – he looked French – and his two beautiful dogs. And we thought we'd be alone.

We walked a long way up a steep hill and found a guesthouse run by a German woman who was clearly unhinged. We ate the worst meal of our lives: just-out-of-the-tin cold beans and sweetcorn, unmentionable boiled potatoes and something that looked like a nappy, but was apparently fish.

'It's always a mistake to eat on land when we're in port,' Michael said, looking at me hard. 'Much better to continue eating on the *bateau*. Don't you think?'

I suppose I did think. The German woman let us 'buy' a shower from her and use her computer to get our emails. I had two from E.C saying that though I am far away I am close to him in his thoughts and that we are still under the same sky. E.C who? Right now my fantasies are about cooking for the lone French man and his two dogs on that pale blue steel boat next to ours.

Two things I wish I'd known about sooner

1 Sprouting seeds, growing shoots, and why bother

This is much easier than you might imagine from the bewildering amount of kit that you see for sale. You don't need any of those three-tiered contraptions that look like budgerigar cages – and could they be any more off putting?

All we did on the boat, as per Jeremy's instructions, was put some seeds in a jam jar (each type of seed gets its own jar, as their sprouting time varies), filled it about half way up with filtered water, punched holes in its lid, so that it didn't get too stuffy in there, and then waited – for about three days. Keep the jar away from direct sunlight, change the water and give the seeds a rinse using a sieve twice a day, which takes about thirty seconds.

We were sceptical at first. Mung beans? Sprouted red lentils? What was the point? The trick is not just to chuck the sprouts at other things – they are pointless lost in a leafy salad – but to handle them as delicacies in their own right. A bowl of seed sprouts mixed together with seaweed flakes and a slug of tamari is a deliciously salty little snack. It satisfies the potato-chip-type of craving, but, unlike crisps, it is, actually, satisfying. Or mix them with some cucumber, cored and cut into chunks, or slivers of raw fennel and Parmesan, then dress them with a light vinaigrette of just a little peppery olive oil, Maldon salt and pepper.

A word about sprouted chickpeas: we ate them raw on the boat and they were good, but they are even better if you blanch them for a few seconds in boiling water.

We sprouted mung beans, green lentils, chickpeas and sunflower and alfalfa seeds on the boat (the latter take longer, but you are rewarded with leafy little shoots rather than just sprouts), but you can sprout pretty much any seed, grain or legume.

I have now learnt a little bit more about sprouting, but all I've done is refine the process slightly. I still sprout things in a jar or pint glass rather than in a germinator, but, after soaking the seeds overnight in plenty of water, then draining them, I now just keep them wet, rather than sitting in water for the rest of the sprouting time. I still rinse them in the morning and evening. And, instead of punching holes in the top of the jam jar, I use a piece of muslin as a lid, secured on to the jar with a rubber band. It makes the rinsing and watering quicker and easier.

2 Paloma coleslaw

The Paloma coleslaw got better and better as the days passed. I would add something that worked one day (parsley, say, or a few pine nuts), and then something that didn't the next (a handful of cooked quinoa, sliced cornichons), and so on. I thought of it as 'The Process of Refining the Coleslaw' and also 'Using Up the Cabbage'.

You have to be careful with coleslaw. Cole means 'cabbage'. Coleslaw is a 'cabbage salad'. Carrot and celeriac are good in a coleslaw, but grated beetroot is a bit sweet, and apple, raisins and celery somehow subtract more than they add; avoid them.

Traditionally, coleslaw is dressed with mayonnaise, but on the boat we preferred it with a fresher dressing of oil and lemon juice. Japanese plum vinegar (with oil) is also good, but I left the soy sauce and Worcester sauce to Toby. Likewise, this salad doesn't keep – the crunch factor is the point.

Chop finely (shred I suppose is the term) equal amounts of **red** and **white cabbage** (white cabbage has a slightly sweeter, nuttier taste than the green variety) and grate about a quarter of this amount of **carrot**. Finely dice half a **red onion**. (Use a whole onion if you are making a lot of coleslaw.) Shredded **celeriac** is a nice addition, but use it modestly – nothing should outshine the cabbage.

Toast a handful of **pumpkin seeds**, **sunflower seeds** and **pine nuts** in a dry pan, tossing them about so that they turn golden brown. The pumpkin seeds will take longest, so put them in the pan for about a minute before adding the others.

Roughly chop a large bunch of **parsley**. For the dressing, mix together three parts good **olive oil** to one part fresh **lemon juice** and season with plenty of **Maldon salt** and freshly ground **black pepper**. Toss everything together extremely well.

The beautiful Aurore

After we'd spent a bit of time on the Azores it was time to sail home. Only Michael, Dave and I didn't want to go home. At all. Plus, it seemed that the boat needed some urgent repairs. We decided to stay. Jeremy and Toby flew back to the States, and Aurore, Michael's girlfriend, flew out to the Azores in their place.

Aurore is a beautiful Italian. She arrived with a tiny suitcase out of which, each day, she pulled new delights: her mother's olive oil in San Pellegrino green bottles, rice flour, essential oils, tiny pieces of white lace which she wore, bra-less, to devastating effect, jewel-coloured bikinis, sarongs from West Africa, Japanese plum vinegar, cashmere sweaters and an emerald scarf. I, meanwhile, developed an unbelievably ugly and uncomfortable rash all over my body.

We spent another month sailing around the nine islands of the Azores and then eight days sailing to Lisbon, where we ended our journey. On top of everything else, Aurore is a fantastic cook. I spent the time we had together on the boat trying to soak up some of her cooking skills –

the way she made a rice salad by mixing rice with fennel, red pepper, ginger and garlic all chopped very small and cooked together at the same time, or the way she cooked cabbage and carrots in vinegar and just a little bit of oil. She often cooked rice with other grains like quinoa or buckwheat, which made the texture of our rice salads more interesting.

Also, when she craved something sweet, she didn't reach for a biscuit, but mixed toasted sunflower seeds with a spoonful of jam or honey so that it made a sort of delicious crunchy jammy-seedy paste.

Aurore's rice and quinoa salad

Use one handful of jasmine or basmati **rice** mixed with **quinoa** for each person. Rinse the rice and quinoa in water a few times before putting it in a saucepan with one and a half times more water than grain. Bring to a simmer and then cook, covered, until the water has evaporated and the rice and quinoa are cooked.

Finely chop about half a **bell pepper** per person (it can be red, green or yellow), one seeded **red chilli**, a bunch of **parsley** (or mint or basil) and a handful of good **olives**. A couple of **anchovies** chopped up are also a good addition. Mix everything together in a large bowl.

Finely chop a large **onion** and, in a frying pan over a low heat, gently fry it in a tablespoon of good **olive oil** and two tablespoons of **water**. Mix the cooked onion with the peppers and the rice and quinoa. Dress with a little more **olive oil** and season with **Maldon salt**, freshly ground **black pepper** and **chilli powder**.

Aurore's sauerkraut

Soak two or three handfuls of **raisins** in hot water for about half an hour. Meanwhile, using a sharp knife, chop a whole **white cabbage** very finely. Drain the raisins and rinse them a few times in fresh water.

Place the chopped cabbage, raisins and two or three handfuls of **pine nuts** in a lidded saucepan. Add 80ml of good **olive oil** and a **bay leaf** and fry, covered, over a low heat for five minutes. Give it a quick stir every now and then so that it doesn't burn. Add 80ml of **umeboshi vinegar** and cook, covered, on a low heat for a long time – the longer the better – but

forty-five minutes to an hour will do it. Give it a stir every few minutes. The vinegar is very salty, so you don't need to add any salt to the mix. If it starts to get too dry add a little water – you want almost all of the liquid to evaporate and be absorbed by the vegetables, so be careful not to add too much.

Chapter three
Learning not to cook.
'Have a boiled egg and
get on with life' (Pops'
philosophy on food)

Mum and the soufflés

There is a picture that hangs in our family kitchen in Somerset. It is a framed illustration for a story on Pop Art, torn out from *The Sunday Times Magazine* by my mother, Polly, over forty years ago. It shows a Lichtenstein-type cartoon blonde holding a can of Campbell's soup in her hand. A big tear is coming out of her eye and a big thought bubble is coming out of her head. In the thought bubble are written the words: 'What *shall* we give Andy for supper.'

When I was little I used to stare at this picture in fascination. I understood that the picture meant something to my mum and dad because Pops' real name is Andy, and I learned that the name also referred to the artist Andy Warhol, but what I could not comprehend was why, even in a universe of games and word play, the woman was so upset. What was the big deal about what you might give Andy, or anyone else, for dinner? Why, on any level at all, was the woman so concerned?

My mum did not worry about what she would give Andy for supper when we were growing up, just as

worrying about what he would feed Polly did not cause Andy too many sleepless nights. Both worked full-time and neither cooked; it was as simple as that. Though both were deeply involved with the house and garden, never mind us, it was someone else – a live-in housekeeper – who did the actual housekeeping. This included the cooking.

'Do you enjoy cooking?' my mum asked me not long ago, genuinely curious.

It's true that when I left England to live in New York I had barely cooked a meal, and when I returned, eight years later, I began obsessively insisting that I cook every single one – often for twelve or fourteen people – so she knew something had gone on. But she was still curious – bemused almost – that I seemed to find cooking a pleasure rather than a chore.

'I *really* enjoy it,' I told her. She shook her head.

'Well...' she said.

'Don't you?' I asked her. 'At all? When you are doing it, don't you find yourself enjoying it? Don't you find it distracting and creative and focusing and relaxing and difficult and easy in all the right ways?'

'I might,' she said. 'I think I'd enjoy it more if everything I made didn't taste like cauliflower cheese.'

That made me laugh, because for years that's exactly what we ate: housekeeper food that tasted of cauliflower cheese. Family meals consisted of white stuff served out of huge ceramic gratin dishes: fish pie, crumble, cottage pie, shepherd's pie, cauliflower cheese and potato dauphinoise. It all tasted the same: big and white, floury and milky and runny. The sort of good solid English nursery food that you often hear people talk longingly about, and which has become fashionable as an antithesis to anything too cheffy or too fushiony or too tall and towery or served in too small a portion, or accompanied by too much of a garnish or too much of any kind of flourish.

'What about a meat pie?' Pops says longingly whenever the subject of what to cook comes up. Meat pie is what he calls shepherd's pie and I rarely cook it when I'm in Somerset, because he eats it so often when I'm not there, cooked to perfection by Jo who, with her husband Ron, looks after us, the house and Pops in particular. Apparently Pops does not tire of meat pie. Or crumble.

'What about crumble?' he said the other day when I announced that I was going to make *Iles flotantes.* 'Oh do let's have crumble.'

But then he ate the soft meringues floating in their custard and when I said, 'Do you still wish I'd made a crumble?' he blushed and gave me a sheepish look. But the next day when Rose did indeed make a crumble I knew what we were all thinking: however flirty and delicious a meringue pudding is, however pleased you are to eat it, and however much it promises and then delivers, the fact remains: nothing, but nothing, beats a good crumble, and the best crumble of all is an apple crumble.

Apple crumble (crumble, crumble, crumble)

Apple crumble is easy, but its specialness can vary. Pops likes lots of fruit and just a little crumble on his plate, but that works just fine because everybody else likes the ratio the other way round. 'Crumble,' my sister Bay always says, 'crumble, crumble, crumble. Is there any more of the crumble bit?' When she gave birth to her son, Billy (who weighed well over ten pounds), a nurse asked her if she wanted dessert after her first post-labour hospital dinner. 'Could I have apple crumble?' Bay asked hopefully. It was what she wanted more than anything in the world. She couldn't; the hospital offered only jelly or ice cream.

Still, however much crumble you want, when you come to make it you have to be careful not to pile it too thickly onto its fruit base, however tempting. The problem then is that though the top browns and the bottom gets nice and soggy from the fruit, the middle bit stays dry and gravelly. What you want is a bit of sog, a bit of crunch and a little bit of something in-between. The best way to do this is to make the crumble in a large relatively flat dish rather than something deeper, and to make sure that your fruit isn't totally 'dry' when you put it in its baking dish (which it won't be if you give it even just a few turns in a saucepan over the heat beforehand).

Serves 6 (if you are greedy like us)
Preheat the oven to 180°C/350°F/gas mark 4. You will need about 700g **apples**. I like to use cookers (Bramley's) because they stay firm and, once a bit of **sugar** is added, taste delicious when cooked. Peel, core and quarter the apples and cut the quarters into halves or thirds, depending on the size of the apple. You want generous bite-sized chunks, bearing in mind that fruit shrinks a bit when cooked. Place the apple chunks in a saucepan or casserole over a low heat with about a tablespoon of water, a good squeeze of **orange juice** (about half a juicy orange) and about 50g of sugar. I often add a couple of **plums** or a handful of **blueberries** or **blackberries** if I've got them, and early in the apple season I do.

Cover the saucepan and let the apples cook gently until they are about half way cooked: that is, until they just begin to soften. Taste and add more sugar if necessary (I usually do). Put the apples into the crumble dish and let them cool while you make the crumble.

You don't really need to weigh amounts when making the crumble because all you are doing is mixing, with your fingertips, **butter**, **flour** and sugar until the texture resembles coarse breadcrumbs. But the way it works out is that you use about equal weights of butter and sugar and a little more than twice as much flour. So, for a six-person crumble use 110g flour, 50g butter and 50g sugar. I usually use light brown sugar, or a mixture of caster and Demerara sugars, but caster or granulated sugar on its own is fine. The butter should be cold but not too hard. Crumble is also good if you use **ground almonds** as part of your flour mix (instead of 110g of plain flour, use 85g of plain flour and 30g of ground almonds).

When the crumble looks like breadcrumbs spread it over the cooled apples. Add a sprinkling of Demerara sugar on top (for extra crunch – and no

one has ever complained about the sweetness). Then bake in the oven for thirty to forty-five minutes, until the topping is cooked and golden and the fruit is just threatening to encroach into the crumble goodness.

If you want to make rhubarb or gooseberry crumble, stew the fruit with sugar (taste to judge how much), but no water, until it is half cooked, then add the crumble.

In fact, Mum, when she cooks, never makes anything floury in a gratin dish. I can say this with certainty because, although Mum is a good cook (she knows how things should taste), she is not interested in range. This is what she cooks: gravy, if I'm not making the roast or if it's Christmas and we are all chipping in; the very occasional fennel purée (once or twice a year); bacon and eggs at the weekend for breakfast when we are all together; and her two staples: roasted red peppers with anchovies and garlic, and a puttanesca sauce to be eaten with pasta, or on its own, or as her vegetarian substitution for the meat component in any and every meal. She makes puttanesca in particular *a lot*. If there is ever any scarcity of capers or anchovies or black olives or tomato purée, get thee to Somerset. We have shelves – shelves and shelves and shelves – of them: in tins and glass jars and tubes and vacuum-packed packages, in brine and salt and olive oil.

Mum makes puttanesca sauce even when it's not needed.

'I'll just make a puttanesca,' she says when I've already started making lunch. 'It'll come in handy,' she explains when I ask her, quite darkly, *why* she is beginning to cook a whole separate meal when lunch has been planned, is vegetable-based, and is already being prepared. I think, for her, puttanesca sauce is a bit like a pot of tea. You don't need a reason to make it: it's just there to be slurped at any time. The first time my boyfriend Nicholas came to Somerset I told him that at some point my mum would make her puttanesca sauce. She greeted him at the door with it. Certainly it is something we can rely on. Invariably, if you go into the larder, sitting below the shelves of puttanesca ingredients there is always a saucepan of Mum's puttanesca sauce. Sitting next to it will be something elaborate and disgusting she has cooked for the dogs.

My mum turns into my great aunt when it comes to cooking for the dogs. Pop's aunt Tiggy, who died fifteen years ago, was English to her bones. She wore tweeds, never married, worked in the home-decorating business, and was passionate about horse racing and Staffordshire Bull Terriers. Hers all had names that began with the letter 'E'. She was a fantastic gardener, a lousy cook, and thought nothing of driving all day to Scotland, say, with the dogs, and then back again. She always returned from a Scottish trip with a Dundee cake or two. She was never ill, and her life was full of amazing adventures, particularly in the war when she was posted to Egypt. When we went to see her she cooked us things we dreaded: tongue, heart and kidneys. Now Mum, a vegetarian, cooks those same things for the dogs. They punch anyone entering the larder with their bovver-boy smell.

'Fuck me I'm a kidney,' the smell shouts. 'I'm a fucking heart. Now Fuck Off.'

And so the puttanesca has turned into a bit of a joke. But not long ago

Mum was vindicated. Rose and Bay and I, and the kids, and Rose's husband and Bay's boyfriend, both called Tom, and Nicholas had planned to leave for London before dinner only we didn't manage it, and so it was with triumph that Mum bought out the puttanesca, made to be ready precisely for such an impromptu meal as this. It was delicious.

Mum's puttanesca sauce

When I asked Mum how she made her puttanesca sauce (and, after all, she is an expert) there was a long silence.

'You can go whistle for Dixie,' she said. 'Sauce is right. You've laughed at me for years, and now you want the recipe!?' She paused for quite a long time so that I could hear her heavy breathing.

'Fine,' she said at last. 'All right. Here is what I do: First of all, I don't use vegetable oil I use good **olive oil**, though not extra virgin.' (It drives Mum mad when we use extra virgin olive oil for cooking. She believes the world is about to run out of olives and so she buys good olive oil in quantity, but hides it in the larder ready for the olive apocalypse. In the meantime, she releases it into the kitchen one bottle at a time labelled boldly with magic marker: 'PRECIOUS olive oil. For dressing ONLY.')

She continues: 'I cut up the **red chillies** and take out the white things' (those would be seeds, Mum) 'And I go completely according to whim on how many chillies I use, but probably two for a good-sized pot of sauce. And I cut up **garlic** – but I make sure the garlic doesn't have brown bits on it.' (Thanks, Mum) '– About two cloves I'd say, and actually I use the pink garlic that I get when I go to Lautrec, which is most important.' (OK, Mum) 'And I put those things in the saucepan with the olive oil, which is hot, and I really keep an eye on it so nothing burns. Then I add a lot of **basil**. Really, a lot of basil. It disappears and later I add a lot more, but this first lot of basil is to flavour the oil. Then I add **black olives**. I use big ones that still have their stones because the ones that you buy with their stones taken out loose their flavour, and I chop them up pretty small. They are already knocked about because of taking the stones out, but I do that with a little machine I've got. Have you got one? Should I get one for you?

And with the olives I put in **anchovies** – two small tins – I don't chop them up but I do add them separately, one by one, and **capers**. How many? About a tablespoon. I cook all that together, quite delicately, and then I add **tomatoes**, enough to make it saucy. It's easy to see how many you need. About ten normal sized ones I should say. I use fresh ones that I peel and chop up. Once the tomatoes are in I always add freshly ground **black pepper**, but never salt because the anchovies and capers are salty enough.

At the same time as the tomatoes I add the second load of basil and a good squeeze of **tomato purée**, either from a tin or the tube. I've found that if I don't add the purée the sauce isn't as rich. I cook it all very slowly for about half an hour. And I've found that it's best cooked the night before. You don't have to of course, but the flavour gets richer, and it sits very happily in its saucepan in the larder over night. You can also keep it in the fridge, practically forever!'

Capers and anchovies are not the only thing Mum stocks in the larder; she has an extensive *batterie de cuisine*, collected over 40 years of mostly not-cooking. Now she buys mostly by mail order, a hobby of hers I fear I may be inheriting.

'It's for peeling tomatoes,' she says as she produces a serrated edged vegetable peeler from an envelope, which I know doesn't work very well because I've already bought – and discarded – one. (Cooks often pretend that they use minimal stuff: 'Me?' they say, 'Just a wooden spoon, a good knife, and a couple of trusted old saucepans for me.' But I've never met anyone who likes to cook who doesn't love kit. It may well not be fancy – *many* wooden spoons, for example – but there's always plenty of it.) Mum, however, is upfront about her extravagance when it comes to kit.

'Do you know how much that fucking thing cost?' she said about a French mandolin I recently unearthed from the larder.

'Ninety fucking pounds. But it doesn't work because it's so fucking badly designed. Ninety pounds. I really mind.' (In fact it works perfectly, and I spend most of the winter julienning celeriac from the garden on it.) On the other hand she is unbelievably thrifty when it comes to saving food.

Nothing is thrown away. Ever. Bacon fat is collected in little jars; dripping sits in the fridge. If leftovers or vegetable peelings can't feed the chickens, then they go to the compost bin. And if something can't go into our garden compost (because it is cooked food, or lemon or orange skins), then it goes to the giant council compost bin, where everything decomposes, except if it's meat or fish bones, and what can't be used for stock goes to the dogs or cats. Recently, when we were in Somerset to pick sloes, Nicholas walked into the kitchen and said in a worried voice,

'But what is that terrible smell?'

'Kidneys,' I said. 'For the dogs.'

But it wasn't. It was, he discovered, a bit of old smoked mackerel skin sitting in a tin bowl waiting to be taken up the lane on a night walk to be left for the foxes.

Plus Mum knows a lot. 'I don't mean to tell you how to suck eggs,' she said to me not long ago when she saw a chicken squeezed into a roasting tray, 'but you need a bigger tin for that chicken.'

Recently, when I wanted to make a chocolate soufflé after remembering the soufflés of my childhood, Mum went for a snuffle in the larder. Because, in fact, over the years, between the cauliflower cheese dishes, we had one housekeeper, Anne, who was a fantastic cook but didn't stay for long, and Wendy who was with us for years and made incredible soufflés incredibly often. When Mum returned to the kitchen she was holding two proper French soufflé tins.

It turns out that when Mum and Pops lived in New York as newly-weds, on the rare occasions that they didn't go out, Mum used to make soufflés. (Question: 'What *shall* we give Andy for dinner?' Between 1968 and 1970 Polly's answer was: 'A cheese soufflé'.) This was news to me. 'Yes,' Mum said, when I stared at her agog. 'I made soufflés. Good ones. The only recipe to use for a soufflé is Julia Child's from *Mastering the Art of French Cooking, Vol. 1*' she continued matter of factly, as if we swapped recipes daily. She put the tins down on the counter in front of me. 'And the only moulds to use are these.'

The proper name for the soufflé tins Mum produced, the ones with the little sticky out handles on their sides, is a 'Charlotte mould', and they are quite hard to find because it's fashionable now to make individual soufflés in small ceramic ramekins. But nothing is like the drama of a single large soufflé – or being chosen to be the first to delve in. I once had lunch at C. Z. Guest's house in Westchester, New York, because I was interviewing her daughter Cornelia. Lunch was a single cheese soufflé brought to the table in a large Charlotte mould just like Mum's. The soufflé came with a green salad, and was served by a uniformed maid wearing white gloves. You can bet that the cook had used Julia Child's recipe.

As soon as Mum showed me the moulds (unused since Wendy left over 20 years ago) a whole chunk of my childhood came whistling back to me.

'Did Wendy use Julia Child's recipe?' I asked Mum.

'Of course she did,' Mum said. 'And she used these tins. The right tin is vital,' Mum said. She gave me a hard look. 'Because of the way it conducts the heat.'

'OK' I said, looking at the tins, one bigger than the other. 'I'll use the smaller one.' (There were only four of us to eat the soufflé.) 'And I'll use Julia Child's recipe.'

Mum kept looking at me. For a long time Mum and Pops didn't take this book on board. I told them I was writing it and they were pleased and then one would say: 'Book? Cooking? What book? Did you tell me about the book? Why didn't you tell us about the book?' But at that moment Mum became very serious. Suddenly she knew all about the book.

'When you are writing about soufflés is it possible for you to advise your readers to use these French tins?'

'Yes,' I said and then I made the soufflé, and here I am, advising.

Charlotte moulds may be hard to find but I know they are worth the hunt. I have now made several chocolate soufflés (I believed Mum about Julia Child, but I still wanted to snuffle about myself and anyway it's no bad thing to make several soufflés in a row; you get to eat them. And a soufflé that doesn't quite work is basically a molten chocolate pudding. Or cold, the next day: a mousse).

A chocolate soufflé has a heavier base than other soufflés, and so is more temperamental than, say, a cheese or orange soufflé, so you need all the help you can get. Use a Charlotte mould and Julia Child.

Her recipe is surprisingly quick and easy – and it really does work, especially if you have an electric whisk or mixer with a whisk attachment to beat the egg whites. It is also worth noting that, although the soufflé will need to be eaten the very moment it comes out of the oven, you can prepare it – egg whites and all – and leave it, uncooked, for up to an hour before putting it in the oven. Just make sure it is in a warm place and cover it with a large bit of foil or cling film to protect it from drafts.

Souffle au chocolat

From *Mastering the Art of French Cooking, Vol. 1*
by Julia Child, Louisette Bertholle and Simone Beck

Chocolate needs special treatment for soufflés because it is heavy. Although the formula in our first version produced a dramatic puff, it was far too fragile. In this new version, you fold the chocolate mixture into a meringue – that is, rather than adding the sugar to the sauce base, you whip it into the egg whites, thereby firming them up. Just this simple change in method gives the soufflé staying power so that instead of collapsing rather rapidly into a pudding, it stays up and retains its primal soufflé character.

For 6 to 8 people

7 ounces or squares of semi-sweet or sweet baking chocolate

$^{1}/_{3}$ cup strong coffee

A small saucepan with cover set in a larger pan of almost simmering water

$^{1}/_{2}$ Tb softened butter

A 2 to 2 $^{1}/_{2}$-quart soufflé dish or straight-sided baking dish 7 $^{1}/_{2}$ to 8 inches in diameter

$^{1}/_{3}$ cup all-purpose flour

A 2-quart saucepan

A wire whip

2 cups milk

3 Tb butter

4 egg yolks

1 Tb pure vanilla extract

6 egg whites ($^{3}/_{4}$ cup)

$^{1}/_{8}$ tsp salt

$^{1}/_{2}$ cup sugar

Powdered sugar in a sieve or shaker

Serving suggestion: 2 cups of sweetened whipped cream, crème anglaise or vanilla ice cream

Preheat the oven to 425 degrees

Place the chocolate and coffee in the small pan, cover, and set in the larger pan of almost simmering water. Remove from heat and let the chocolate melt while you proceed with the recipe.

Smear the inside of the dish with butter. Surround with a collar of buttered aluminium foil (double thickness) to reach 3 inches above the rim of the dish. Set out all the rest of the ingredients called for.

Measure the flour into the saucepan. Start whisking in the milk by dribbles at first to make a perfectly smooth cream; rapidly whisk in the rest. Add the butter, and stir over moderate heat until boiling; boil, stirring, for 2 minutes. Remove from heat and beat 1 minute or so to cool slightly.

One by one, whisk the egg yolks into the hot sauce, then the smoothly melted chocolate, and finally the vanilla.
(*) If you are not continuing within 5 to 10 minutes, lay a sheet of plastic wrap directly on top of the sauce to prevent a skin from forming.

Beat the egg whites and salt in a separate bowl until soft peaks are formed. Then, by sprinkles, beat in the sugar and continue until stiff shining peaks are formed.

Scrape the chocolate mixture into the side of the egg white bowl; delicately fold them together. Turn the soufflé mixture into the prepared mold and set on a rack in the lower level of the preheated oven. Turn thermostat down to 375 degrees.

In 35 to 40 minutes, when the soufflé is well risen and the top has cracked, rapidly sprinkle the surface with powdered sugar; continue baking another 5 to 10 minutes. Soufflé is still creamy at the centre when a skewer plunged down through a surface crack comes out slightly coated. It is fully done and will stand up well (if that is how you like it) when the skewer comes out clean. Serve at once with one of the suggestions listed.
(*) When turned into its baking dish, the soufflé may be covered loosely with a sheet of oil and set in a draft-free part of the kitchen for an hour or more before being baked.

89

School dinners and housekeepers

Mostly we didn't eat soufflés. Mostly we ate solidly, stolidly and well. We had a vegetable garden and fruit trees and so ate seasonally and healthily – fast food doesn't exist in the countryside – but nothing we ate, other than raw vegetables and fruit, had any real taste. Food was just there at meal times: how it got there was pretty much taken for granted. Was cooking an effort? Was it stressful or joyful? Were the results a disappointment or a triumph? Those sorts of questions didn't occur to us. We helped lay the table and clear away and we grew closer to some of the housekeeper's than others, but it didn't occur to us to get involved with any cooking.

When we went to boarding school, once we hit nine, the non-ness of food was only reinforced. Meals at school were universally dreaded, and the management took a certain pride in the fact that the food was revolting – as if good food would turn us all into mini Prince Regents. The gardens of the school were magnificent, dogs accompanied teachers to lessons, and our head mistress, whom we called Sarah, taught us to ride and gave us our Latin lessons. At night she said good-bye to each and every pupil with a handshake. When she taught, her black whippet, Spry, would lie sprawled on a classroom desk covered with her mistress's green Husky jacket. Sometimes Sarah asked Spry to watch us while she left a lesson to deal with some pressing matter. If we misbehaved – she said she only had to look at Spry to know – she made us do a little dance in the corner of the classroom.

What matter food with such riches about? Food was simply to be got through and finished; plates had to be clean; debris wasn't allowed. Rubbish Pie, served every Sunday evening, was made with the week's leftovers (bacon rind, globs of watery old scrambled egg, baked beans, bits of old liver) and was one of the school's specialities.

Like school, what was important in terms of our housekeepers was their company, and the atmosphere they cast in the kitchen. Wendy did everything: the cooking, the housekeeping, the ironing *and* she was my mum's typist and secretary. She was with us for years and became part of our family, and we still talk about her. Before coming to us she had been married to Kevin, a watch-maker, while she was with us her boyfriend was Arthur the plumber, and when she left us she married Ronnie, a butcher. I call that a full flush.

After Wendy came Liz, a strict vegan. She had an enormous pet pig called Duncan, a herd of sheep who responded to their given names, and she turned her flat into a menagerie. Dogs and rabbits and cats and guinea pigs shared the same beds and baskets, and there was never any upset. Liz was straightforward as a person, which made her good, reassuring company. I remember sitting on the front door step and complaining about the terrible shortness and thickness of my legs.

'What's wrong with them?' she asked, genuinely bewildered at my moaning. 'They work perfectly well, don't they?' But she didn't sound sharp when she said it, just sensible. It was easy to be in the kitchen with Liz, unlike Jane, who was with us before Wendy and who was also vegetarian, as well as a Quaker. She had a son called Luke who played snooker, and two Irish Wolfhounds. We were scared of Jane. Her crumble tasted like gravel, Pops said. We weren't at all scared of Donna though, who arrived later.

Donna moved in when I was nine and just going away to boarding school. Rose was way ahead and had already put in two years away. But Bay, who was still at home, and Donna became very close. They wore matching Dr. Scholl sandals, which were the only flat shoes Donna could wear because her arches were so high (she was only comfortable in stilettos she said), and both spoke in a soft West Country accent.

Donna was a single mum with a small son called Ben, and she'd barely cooked a meal before coming to live with us, but that didn't seem to worry anyone and certainly her shepherd's pie was as good as any of the others.

'Cooked a meal? Donna?' Mum said when I asked her recently if my memory was right. 'Donna hadn't ever eaten a meal.'

Donna had dark shiny hair with purple streaks through it, which she used to crimp. And she wore very tight jeans with T-shirts that revealed her wonderful bosom. She was on probation for some crime or other, and her probation officer, who came to check up on her once a week, had a tin leg. She began sleeping with him immediately. He was her 'good' boyfriend, but she also had a 'bad' one, who stayed in town. She told us she liked them both the same, but 'in different ways,' and that seemed to make sense.

We *adored* Donna and I'm sure we liked her cooking because we were so relaxed around her. She may not have understood ingredients (she once dared me to eat a raw, peeled potato and I got half way through before Mum found us. 'What are you doing, you pillocks?' Mum shouted. 'Raw potato is poisonous!'), but though she cursed and swore at food when things went wrong, she wasn't profoundly resentful or in a hurry when she cooked. She didn't punish food in the way that a later housekeeper, Sonia, did. Sonia's trick was to make enough food for twenty. She only ever used the party-sized gratin dish, however few of us were eating.

Think of shepherd's pie. Shepherd's pie is nearly always fine, even when you're confronted with too much of it (and even when it tastes a bit like cauliflower cheese). But *fine* is a let down, really, and bland is certainly unacceptable when you are making something so straightforward and unpretentious. This is what Jane Grigson says about shepherd's pie:

'Anyone can cook steak. It takes a modest and generous skill to turn cheaper cuts of meat into something good.'

How do you make it into something good? Well, you take care with it. You buy good, fresh mince from a butcher (ask them to mince some beef or lamb, or a mixture of both, in front of you) on the day that you are going to cook it. Cook the mince soon after buying it as it looses its freshness very quickly. Then you cook the pie in stages, rather than throwing it all together.

Shepherd's pie

This is a combination of what Jane Grigson says with some of what Jo, who lived with us, does. Pops says Jo makes the best meat pie he's ever tasted – and he's tasted a few.

Serves 6

3 tbsp of vegetable oil
600g lean minced beef
    and/or lamb
75g, plus 1 tbsp butter
1 tbsp olive oil
large onion, finely chopped
2 garlic cloves, finely chopped
largish carrot, finely chopped
1 celery stick, finely chopped
1 tsp fresh thyme leaves
1 tbsp cornflour

1 tbsp tomato purée
250ml red wine
2 tsp Worcestershire sauce
450ml beef stock
1 tbsp chopped parsley
750g potatoes
200ml milk
small handful grated Cheddar
    cheese
1 tbsp Parmesan

1 Preheat the oven to 200°C/400°F/gas mark 6.

2 Heat the vegetable oil in a frying pan until it's almost smoking and cook the mince in small batches stirring each batch until it is well coloured. Drain it in a colander while you get on with the next stage, which is the sweating of the vegetables.

3 Melt the tablespoon of butter and the olive oil in a medium sized saucepan and stir in the onion, garlic, carrot, celery and thyme leaves. Cover them with a butter wrapper or a piece of greaseproof paper the same size as the inside of the saucepan (a cartouche) and put the lid on the saucepan. Let the vegetables cook very gently on a low heat for about ten minutes. You want them to release their flavours without turning brown, so the low heat is crucial.

94

4 Raise the heat and add the cooked mince, the cornflour and tomato purée. Cook for a few minutes, stirring occasionally, then slowly add the red wine, Worcestershire sauce and beef stock. Season well, especially with lots of black pepper and add the chopped parsley. Bring to the boil, then lower the heat and simmer for about fifty minutes, until the liquid has thickened. Leave to cool.

5 While the mince is simmering and thickening, boil the potatoes in their skins, in plenty of salted water. When they are cooked (about fifteen to twenty minutes), drain and peel them. Then, making sure they are really dry, return them to the pan (make sure that is dry, too) and heat them just a little bit.

6 Now mash them. Melt the 75g butter and heat the milk, and add them both to the potatoes. Continue mashing until you have a smooth but firm mash.

7 Transfer the mince mixture into a suitable cooking dish and cover with the mashed potato. Rough it up with a fork to give it a bit of texture, then sprinkle it with grated Cheddar cheese and Parmesan.

8 Bake in the oven for ten minutes, then reduce the heat to 180°C/350°F/gas mark 4 and bake for a further forty-five minutes (the high temperature at the beginning helps the top to brown).

Donna stopped being our housekeeper when we moved from Gloucestershire to a falling down farmhouse in Somerset. The advantage of Somerset was its location – it meant we had space, and a view of the hills and woods uninterrupted by either road or telegraph pole. It also meant that my parents could build what they wanted, and what they wanted, they said, was a house that worked like a concertina. That, instead of heating draughty corridors and too many staircases, they wanted a place that could expand and shut down easily as we all came and went.

Our coming and going has always been an integral part of the house. When we first moved in, in 1982, all three of us were at boarding school. And now, twenty-six years later it is still the place where we all converge, and frequently. 'The house will have a sprung wooden dance floor,' we were promised, and so it does. It has rooms for friends and children; places to work quietly and places to meet noisily and one of those places, of course, is the kitchen, which is where, like most families, we spend most of our time.

And yet cooking was never a part of our lives. It wasn't frowned on, it just wasn't talked about or considered – and that wasn't considered an absence. Now that I cook such a lot and find, most of the time, such relief in it, and not just that, find it to be such an easy way of negotiating so many things that are otherwise quite complicated and mysterious – family life, friendships, living with someone, dealing with the blues, taking responsibility, making a home – I simply cannot imagine that it wasn't a gaping hole in our lives. But it wasn't.

I think that that is partly why it has taken a while for my parents to realise that I don't just cook for the sake of producing a meal. I really *cook*. I earn part of my living writing about cooking. My mother's best friend is a writer herself and a woman of towering intellect. When she heard I was working on a book she was pleased.

'What sort of book?' she asked me, all ears. I told her it was about learning to cook. 'Oh,' she said, suddenly cross. 'No,' she continued. 'That's not what I had in mind at all.'

I grew up thinking that cooking was something other people did. Meals were the point of restaurants and cafés, and cooking was something you did quickly in order to refuel and get on with the business of life. You made yourself an omelette before going out dancing, or buttered some toast before jumping on the subway to rush to the office or workplace. You enjoyed food when you were sitting in a French café eating apple tart or a glamorous New York restaurant ordering sea bass or a London Chinese trying Bird's Nest Soup.

And so I didn't cook. Why would I? I wanted to have adventures, not be a housekeeper, and so I learnt not to cook. To get around it and have fun doing so. Restaurants! Eggs! Cheap cafés! Bowls of soup on knees! Youth! Nightclubs! Scaling a volcano! Rafting down a river! A harum-scarum life without apron strings! I had no idea that cooking itself offered its own kind of adventure. It was either something that was done quickly between the laundry and the ironing, or the province of chefs in professional kitchens hidden away and off limits behind swinging doors.

In fact we did have one housekeeper, apart from Wendy, who was a good cook. Anne had trained at Leith's cookery school, and though she had never worked as a professional cook, and was really too young and glamorous and neurotic to be a housekeeper buried in the countryside, she was looking for a stop-gap job while she recovered from a divorce.

The first meal Anne made us was a sesame beef salad with mushrooms, mange tout and wild rice, and it was a revelation. It also only added to my sense of good food as being entirely

98

mysterious and well beyond my ken. Beef? We *never* ate beef, except in a burger or cottage pie. We ate a lot of lamb and chicken but never, ever beef. Sesame was just a random word without meaning. Salad had always meant lettuce. Mushrooms, mange tout and rice we knew. We didn't dread the meal, it just sounded unlikely.

The beef came in small strips and the sauce, a little sticky and delicious, was unlike anything we'd ever tasted – *it actually tasted*. There were onions in it, but they were soft, and the mushrooms and mange tout and the beef were the salad and it all came on a bed of wild rice, which tasted a bit like nuts. It became the meal we wanted Anne to cook the most, though it was really a party dish because sirloin beef is not an everyday ingredient in terms of any kind of budget, and because Anne told us it took a long time to make, which we didn't wonder. There was no doubt about it: you had to be a trained cook to make something like that.

Not long ago, in a bookshop, I spotted a giant tome called *Leith's Cookery Bible*. I remembered Anne, her Leith's training and her sesame beef,

and so I looked up the recipe. There it was. Now I make it often and it isn't hard at all, though it is quite expensive, and you need to start marinating it the night before. I make it with normal basmati, rather than wild rice.

Sesame beef salad, adapted from *Leith's Cookery Bible*
Serves 6

Buy a **sirloin steak** that weighs about 450g and is 5cm thick, and remove any fat from it. The night before cooking it make up a marinade by combining two finely sliced (not diced) **onions**, five tablespoons of **dry sherry**, five tablespoons of **light soy sauce** (or whatever soy sauce you've got will be fine), three tablespoons of **sesame oil** and plenty of freshly ground **black pepper**. Put the steak into the marinade (a freezer bag is good for this) and make sure the marinade coats the steak really well before putting it into the refrigerator overnight.

The next day, make a dressing by whisking together six tablespoons of **grape seed** or groundnut oil, three tablespoons of **white wine vinegar**, a tablespoon of **Dijon mustard** and a teaspoon of **clear honey**.

Now you are ready to cook the beef. Strain the marinade and separate the onions and beef. Keep everything. In a frying pan heat about a tablespoon of **olive oil** until it is very hot, and then brown the steak on both sides. Cook it for as long as you like your steak cooked, which I think should be hardly at all (a couple of minutes on each side). Once it is done, take it out of the pan and put it on a wire rack to cool.

Now put the fine slices of onions that were once part of the marinade into the frying pan and cook over a medium heat until they are soft and golden. Lift them out of the pan and put them into the dressing you have made. Add 225g of sliced **button mushrooms** and the reserved marinade to the frying pan and cook until the marinade becomes syrupy. Add this to the dressing and let it all get cold. Briefly cook the **mange tout** in boiling water until they are just done, then drain them and add them to the dressing.

When everything is cold cut the steak into thin strips, add to the dressing and toss everything together. Serve with rice and perhaps a salad of baby spinach leaves.

London to Somerset

The housekeeper years did not last forever. Nor did boarding school. Rose left hers when she was fifteen and went to live with our mum in her small flat in London. I followed a year later, and we moved into a house in Hammersmith. A year after that Bay arrived. For the first time in years we all lived together on a daily basis and got to know each other properly, which meant that we fought a lot and became, very quickly, very close. Every Friday after school Mum drove all of us to Somerset, which was 'home,' as opposed to London, which was 'London,' and every Friday night in Somerset we ate fish pie.

If you are Catholic, which we are, you eat fish on Fridays, and we ate ours with a lot of white sauce underneath a lot of mash. The merit of the pies varied, depending on which housekeeper we had at the time: Liz's was fine, Sonia's huge and disgusting, Donna's I can't even remember, Wendy's must have been efficient and good, and Anne's, no doubt, was delicious, but her sesame beef was so dazzling that it had blinded us to anything else that she might cook.

Fish pie, like shepherd's pie, but more so, depends on who is cooking it and how much they give a shit. A good recipe helps a lot. I use Mark Hix's from his brilliant book *Fish etc.*.

Mark's very good recipe for fish stock

Place two kilos of **fish bones** and **trimmings** (your fishmonger will usually give these to you for free) in a large pan with two **onions**, two **leeks** (make sure they are well rinsed), and half a head of **celery**, all coarsely chopped. Add half a **lemon**, a teaspoon of **fennel seeds**, twenty **black peppercorns**, a **bay leaf**, a few **thyme sprigs**, a handful of **parsley** (stalks and all) and a pinch of **salt**. Cover all these ingredients with one and a half litres of **cold water** and bring to the boil. Skim well and simmer gently, skimming from time to time.

Remember: unlike other stocks, fish stock is time sensitive. If you let it cook for too long it will taste bitter. Strain the stock and season it to taste, though don't add too much salt if you might be reducing the stock down for using in another recipe.

Mark Hix's fish pie
from *Fish etc.* by Mark Hix

As Mark says, this basic recipe (although there is nothing basic about it) can be varied endlessly depending on what fish is available, but it is always a good idea to include some smoked fish and, apart from salmon, to avoid oily fish. I usually use smoked haddock and sometimes mussels instead of prawns (steaming a kilo or so in a little white wine and using the strained juices as a quick substitute for fish stock).

Serves 4–6

500ml fish stock (see page 101)
2 tbsp dry vermouth
large onion, finely chopped
fennel bulb, cored,
    finely chopped
250g white fish (such as
    pollack fillet), skinned,
    all bones removed
175g salmon fillet, skinned,
    all bones removed
175g smoked fish (such as
    smoked undyed haddock),
    skinned, all bones removed
150g peeled raw prawns

50g butter
50g flour
175ml double cream
2 tbsp Dijon mustard
1 tsp anchovy essence
2 tbsp mixed green herbs
    (fresh parsley, chervil, dill
    or a combination)

for the potato topping
1.5kg of potatoes
90g butter
a slosh of milk
freshly grated Parmesan

1 Place the fish stock and vermouth in a large saucepan and bring to the boil. Add the onion and fennel, and cook gently for eight minutes.

2 Cut the fish into rough 3cm chunks. Add the chunks and the prawns to the stock and vegetables, and poach gently for two minutes. Drain, over a bowl, in a colander, saving the cooking liquid. Leave to cool.

3 Now make the sauce for the pie: melt the butter in a heavy-based saucepan over a low heat. Stir in the flour and cook gently for a minute. (This is called a roux, and is the base for many sauces.)

4 Gradually add the reserved fish poaching liquid; stirring well until it is all added and the mixture is smooth. If you add it too quickly the sauce will be lumpy, which you don't want. Bring to the boil and simmer gently for thirty minutes.

5 Add the double cream and continue to simmer for ten minutes or so, until the sauce has a thick consistency. Stir in the mustard and anchovy essence. Season with salt and freshly ground white pepper (black is fine, too) if you feel it needs it (it probably does). Leave to cool for fifteen minutes.

6 Preheat the oven to 180°C/350°F/gas mark 4. Gently fold the cooked fish, prawns, onion and fennel pieces with the mixed green herbs into the sauce. Spoon all this into a large pie dish, leaving a gap of about 3cm from the top for the potato. Leave this to set for about half an hour, which means that when it's time, the mash will sit happily on the sauce rather than sinking into it.

7 While you're waiting, boil the potatoes in their skins in salted water. When they are done (fifteen to twenty minutes), drain and peel them, then make sure that they are really dry by putting them back into the saucepan over a very low heat for a moment or two. Melt the butter and warm the milk, then add both to the potatoes and mash together. Season with salt and freshly ground black pepper and then spread onto the fish mixture with a spatula.

8 Bake for half an hour, then scatter over some freshly grated Parmesan and bake for another ten to fifteen minutes until the top of the pie is golden.

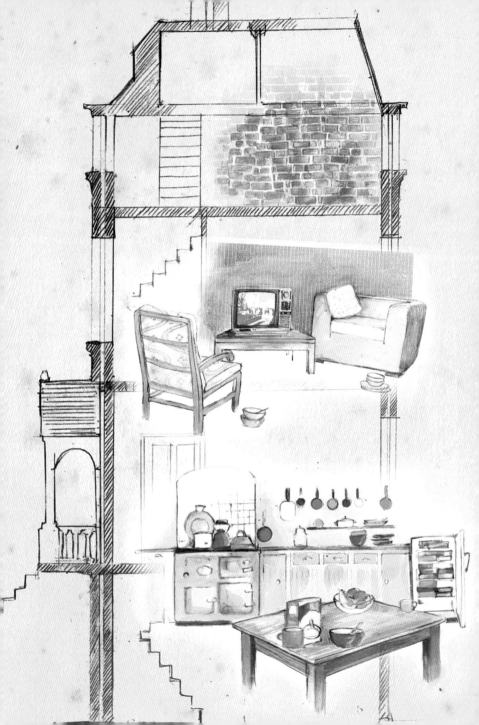

In London we lived in what had been a set of Victorian artists' studios piled one on top of the other. Mum converted the biggest studio, at the bottom of the house, into a kitchen and put an Aga in it so that it would feel like home. This also solved the problem of meals. If you have an Aga no one really has to cook because it does that for you.

'What shall we have for dinner?' Between 1987 and 1993 the answer was: 'Things you shove into the Aga.' We lived off baked potatoes and delicious things that came in packages from Marks and Spencer, our favourites being lasagne, sole goujons and calamari.

'Who has eaten all the fucking goujons?' was regularly shouted out by someone with their head deep inside the fridge.

Mum did all of the shopping – certainly all the big stuff – and she set up an account for us at the local delicatessen so that we could buy bread and hummus and taramasalata and olives. We also ate an obscene amount of fruit each day (we thought nothing of putting away three or four oranges, a couple of apples and a large bunch of grapes between getting back from school and eating supper, or between supper and bed). To avoid rows, Mum quite often divided the grapes into three portions, one for each sister. We were fifteen, sixteen and eighteen years old. Spoiled or what?

I don't ever eat precooked meals now. If I'm feeling lazy I eat bread and cheese or a bowl of rice and peas or I'll happily buy a sandwich. But I do sometimes long for the food of my adolescence: those days when we yelled at each other from the top of the house that the baked potatoes were ready or ate huge bowls of cornflakes while sat, crammed up together in front of the TV, thrilled that *The Breakfast Club* was on for the 800th time.

Sole goujons

I began making goujons only recently, after Rory O'Connell showed my friend Thomas and I how he cooks them. I've never liked deep frying things in a large saucepan full of hot oil.

But of course you *can* do it: you heat the oil in a tall saucepan until it is 190°C/375°F, or however hot the recipe tells you it should be, and you check the temperature either using a thermometer or by doing the bread test, which is when you throw a small piece of bread into the oil and if it comes to the surface nicely golden and fried then the oil is hot enough. But I'd rather not bother. Not long ago, Rose made chips and the oil bubbled over when we weren't paying attention (luckily we weren't cooking on gas). For hours all we did was mop up very hot oil and shout at the children to 'Get Out Of The Kitchen'. It felt like you could fry an egg on any of the kitchen surfaces for the rest of the night. I thought: fuck chips and goujons and those delicious matchstick courgettes in batter, I'll do without.

But then Rory showed us his deep fat fryer when we were in Cork cooking with him, and he made sole goujons for us, which he served with tomato salsa and an aïoli, and it was all so good that the very next day Thomas and I went out and bought a deep fat fryer for ourselves (they cost about thirty quid) because we were about to spend a week together in Kerry. We deep fried every day and loved it more and more. Now I want to buy a deep fat fryer for everyone I love. But maybe that's too weird.

Rory's spiced goujons with tomato salsa and an aïoli

You can replace the sole with brill, turbot or squid. A firm-textured fish is essential, so that the goujons don't fall apart and stay crispy. You can prepare pretty much everything ahead of time and then fry the fish at the last minute. (If I'm cooking squid in the deep fat fryer, I follow a slightly different, quicker, recipe without sesame seeds.)

Serves 4

You need three **Dover sole** (or other fish), about 625g each, skinned, filleted and trimmed. Cut each fillet in half horizontally, then each half into three vertical fingers. To make the spiced flour combine 150g **plain flour**, 1½ teaspoons of **salt**, three tablespoons **sesame seeds**, two teaspoons **white pepper** (or black if you don't have white), two teaspoons **chilli powder** and two teaspoons **curry powder**.

Before you fry the goujons prepare the aïoli and tomato salsa. Aïoli is like a thin, garlicky, pink mayonnaise, which you make in the food processor so it's dead easy (the various ingredients means that it emulsifies quickly). Combine, in the bowl of a food processor: two **egg yolks**, a tablespoon of thick **tomato purée**, a tablespoon of chopped **garlic**, a teaspoon of **white wine vinegar**, 75ml of **fish stock** or lobster water if you've got it (if you haven't just leave it out), a teaspoon of **Dijon mustard**, two finely chopped **anchovies**. (If they are salted, and if possible they should be, give them a good wash under the tap and peel each fillet away from its spine.) Turn the processor on to give the ingredients a blitz and, with the machine still running, slowly pour in 200ml of **sunflower or ground nut oil** and process until you have a smooth sauce. Once it is done, season with **salt** and freshly ground **black pepper** and **lemon juice**, to taste. Add three tablespoons of chopped **coriander** and reserve in a small bowl.

Now for the tomato salsa, if you are making it, and it is only worth making in summer, when you can get very good, tasty tomatoes. (Forget about it during the rest of the year unless you live somewhere hot.) Dice one large white or red **onion**, and 450g of very good, ripe **tomatoes** so that the dice are all about the same size – about 1cm square. Make sure you use all of the tomato. In raw tomato dishes the skin and seeds are most flavourful. Finely chop one seeded **red chilli** and four sprigs of fresh **coriander** and crush, using some **salt** and the flat of your knife, one large clove of **garlic**. Mix everything together and season with **Maldon salt**, freshly ground **black pepper** and **sugar**, to taste.

Now you are ready to cook your lovely goujons. Heat the oil (vegetable or ground nut oil that is) in your deep fat fryer (or a large saucepan) until it tells you that it has reached 190°C/375°F. Have some **milk** in a bowl ready and dip the goujons in the milk and then in the spiced flour so that they are evenly covered all over. Deep fry them in two batches until they are golden brown – this takes about two minutes per batch. Then drain them on kitchen paper and serve immediately on warmed plates with the aïoli and the tomato salsa (or not).

Tomato and basil lasagne
adapted from *Living and Eating*
by Annie Bell and John Pawson

This is a wonderful recipe, because instead of a béchamel sauce (which I'm not mad about, it being white and floury) you use mozzarella and a really good tomato sauce. Not that I sought out a béchamel-less lasagne on purpose. God forbid I shy away from an ingredient. I made this just because it sounded good, and was vegetarian (I first made it when I was giving a dinner for a vegetarian from New York). I've never cooked any other lasagne since discovering it, and everyone I've ever made it for, except the New Yorker (who doesn't cook) has asked me for the recipe, which isn't mine, it's Annie Bell's.

Serves 6

1.3kg beefsteak tomatoes
4 tbsp good extra virgin
    olive oil
an onion, peeled and finely
    chopped
4 garlic cloves, peeled and
    finely chopped
2 tbsp tomato purée,
75ml red wine,
a bay leaf

2 sprigs thyme
1 tsp caster sugar
250g dried egg lasagne
3 buffalo mozzarella cheeses
    (350g in total), diced
75g Parmesan cheese, freshly
    grated
8 large basil leaves, torn in
    half

1 First make the tomato sauce by coring, peeling and coarsely chopping the beefsteak tomatoes. Remove their skins by putting them in as small a container as they'll fit in (I often use a measuring jug), pouring boiling water over them and counting to ten slowly – the skins should slip off easily.

2 Heat three tablespoons of the olive oil in a medium sized saucepan over a moderate heat. Add the onion and let it sweat for a few minutes until it is soft and translucent.

3 Add the garlic and stir around with the onion for a moment or two before adding the chopped tomatoes, tomato purée, red wine, bay leaf and sprigs of thyme. Bring everything to a simmer and cook over a low heat for half an hour, stirring occasionally.

4 Remove the thyme and bay leaf before beating the sauce to a slushy purée using a wooden spoon.

5 Add the caster sugar and season with Maldon salt and freshly ground black pepper. That's your sauce and it's a very good basic tomato sauce for anything from eating very simply over pasta to using in dishes like aubergine Parmigiano.

6 Preheat the oven to 190°C/375°F/gas mark 5 and use a 28cm by 20cm by 6cm baking dish. Cover the base of the dish with some tomato sauce, then add a layer of lasagne, cover that with tomato sauce, scatter over some mozzarella and Parmesan and dot with a couple of torn basil leaves. Repeat these layers using the remaining ingredients. You should have four layers of pasta in all. Finish with tomato sauce and cheese, omitting basil from the final top layer. Instead, drizzle the remaining tablespoon of olive oil over the surface and cover with foil. You can prepare the lasagne to this point in advance and chill it for up to twelve hours until you need it.

7 Bake the lasagne in the oven for twenty minutes, then remove the foil and bake for another twenty-five minutes until the top is golden and bubbling. Serve straight away.

Chapter four
New York living.
When I learnt that food has flavour, and that cooking can be a pleasure

Nell, my New York family and a DJ called Fancy

I went to New York on a whim when I was 23 years old and stayed there for nearly eight years. I had enormous luck. In the space of a week I found work as a journalist, a place to stay, and made a true friend. It was *a bit* more complicated than that, but not much. Work as a journalist is not the same as a full-time job (that came later), and to supplement the short pieces I wrote for American *Vogue* I worked for an artist called Diana Michener. It was through Diana, an extraordinarily generous woman, that I met Nell. And it was through Nell that I got to know New York; through Nell that I met Michael, the skipper of the boat I would later sail home across the Atlantic in; through Nell that I met Rose Gray, who gave me my first cooking lesson; and through Nell that I met many other people who became important to me in New York, and indeed my life beyond the city.

I owe a lot to Nell, not least a great many delicious meals. Nell has a Louise Brooks hairdo in red, which is always shiny, and the legs I would most like to have in the world: perfect dancer's legs that her body sits on squarely. But her legs are nothing to her wit. But then Nell is a dancer, as well as a writer, journalist, and mother, and, when I first met her, she was running, with her partner Eamon, two restaurants and had just finished running a nightclub, that was reckoned, in its heyday – and its heyday was ten years long – to be the best in the world. It was called Nell's.

I met Nell at a party thrown by Diana. There was a magician at the party who made a twenty-dollar bill vanish and reappear on the other side of the room inside a lemon, but he was nothing compared with Nell, who made me, and everyone else in the room, laugh all night.

'Come to dinner on Thursday,' she said to me, and I did.

Dinner was at Nell and Eamon's beautiful Eastern and Oriental Restaurant, which had a small bar and dance floor below its dining room. I had dinner with Nell at E & O almost every Thursday, and at each dinner I'd meet two or three people who would invite me to another dinner (New Yorkers are generous like that) and thus, over sea bass wrapped in banana leaves and steamed with ginger and coriander, I formed a New York life.

Steamed sea bass wrapped in banana leaves

When you went to dinner with Nell at E & O you never quite knew who might to be sitting next to you – in my first few weeks I met an art critic, a nightclub hostess, a DJ, a film director, a carpenter, a scientist, several writers and artists, a set designer, a landscape gardener, a gossip columnist, a fireman, a welder and a drag queen – nor quite what you might be eating, as Nell ordered an array of dishes for the whole table. The climax of the meal was always a whole fish, usually a sea bass, which came to the table still wrapped in banana leaves.

Serves 4

You will need a **sea bass** that weighs about 800g. Any Asian supermarket will sell **banana leaves** (they come in packets of more than you will need and, unfortunately, keep for days rather than weeks, but they aren't expensive), and the best way to steam a fish is to use a Chinese bamboo steamer that comes with a lid and fits over a saucepan. For a single large fish you will need the larger sized steamer.

It is an inexpensive and invaluable piece of equipment, and if you buy more than one you can stack them on top of each other. (If you don't have a steamer, you can bake the fish, wrapped in its leaves – or make it into an aluminium-foil parcel – in a preheated hot oven at 200°C/400°F/gas mark 6.)

To make the paste to brush over the fish you will need: four cloves of **garlic**, four fresh **green chillies**, four **coriander stems** and **roots**, a teaspoon of **salt** and a 2cm-piece of **ginger**, peeled and chopped. Using either a mortar and pestle or a food processor, crush or blend all the ingredients together.

Add a tablespoon of **sugar**, two tablespoons of **fish sauce** (nam pla), and four tablespoons of **lime juice**, which is the juice of about four limes. Blend until all the sugar has dissolved and you have a smoothish paste.

Make sure the fish is clean by giving it a wash and then dry it using kitchen paper. With a sharp knife, score both sides three or four times and brush the paste all over the fish, making sure it gets into the gashes you have made. If you have time let the fish marinate in the paste for an hour or so.

Meanwhile, prepare the banana leaf to wrap around the fish. To make it more pliable, you need to blanch the leaf first, otherwise it rips as soon as you try to fold it. It will be too big for a saucepan as it is, so lower it into a large pan of boiling water, as if you were cooking long spaghetti. It needs only moments in the boiling water to soften. Remove and let it cool and dry for a few minutes before handling it.

Now you will be able to wrap the fish in the leaf, as if it were a parcel. You need to leave room for air to circulate inside the parcel, so don't wrap it up too tightly, but at the same time make sure that it is secure. Tuck the edges of the parcel underneath the fish; the weight of the fish will hold the folds in place.

Place your green parcel in the steamer over a saucepan of boiling water. (If you are baking the fish, place the parcel on a hot baking tray in the preheated oven.) Cook for ten to fifteen minutes, depending on the thickness of your fish. The banana leaves mean that it takes a little longer than an unwrapped fish (ten to twelve minutes). Insert a skewer into the centre of the fish, and when the tip comes out hot, the fish is cooked. Obviously, be careful with the hot metal.

Before I arrived in New York I'd never eaten Thai or Vietnamese food, but then again there was so much I hadn't tried. Oh my God, I was fresh. And naïve. I was 23 years old, which is fine if you are hanging out with other 23-year-olds, but the people I met in New York were mostly older than me and a lot more experienced. I liked that. I wasn't chic or powerful or thin or glamorous, but I *was* young and I was very determined to have adventures: to be festive and up for things and without neurosis, to be no trouble whatsoever, and to more than sing for my supper.

I thought: I'll go home and stop living in New York when it stops being razzle-dazzle and filled with fun and parties *all* the time. I wore a party dress of some description every day and night. One of them, in green silk, was both low-cut and backless. '*But this low cut?*' I remember thinking one night, as I hoisted my endlessly escaping bosom back into place. It was only when I got home at the end of the night that I realised I had been wearing the dress back-to-front. That sums up a good deal about how I presented myself back then: I spilled out a lot.

I dated a DJ called Fancy who lived in a loft in the Lower East Side with a performance artist room-mate who cycled around the loft late at night wearing nothing but a cape, a thong, a pair of socks and enormous silver clogs. Fancy, meanwhile, wore a frilly shirt and a tuxedo suit. Every day. He and the performance artist didn't have a kitchen of any description in their loft, but that didn't matter because they rarely ate.

I ate well. I discovered Japanese and Korean food. I ate a lot of steamed spinach and grilled fish, which is what you order if you are a woman and taken to a chic New York restaurant. I ate cheap Chinese lunches in a canteen in China Town with another boyfriend, a man called Terence who I refused to get keen on, because he, unlike so many of the others, was willing to get keen on me. Oh, there were a lot of fly-by-nights whom I presented myself to wrapped in fucking tinsel more or fucking less.

But Terence was gentle and sweet and somewhat depressed and because he was somewhat depressed he dressed in bright colours. Never mind that I got myself up in leopard and zebra print every night, when I saw him arrive one morning at my door wearing yellow dungarees and red clogs my expression must have demanded an explanation.

'I know, Darling,' Terence said. 'But I'm hanging on. I need all the help I can get.'

Sometimes I was hanging on, too. Sometimes I was lonely and sometimes I felt knocked around, which was no wonder considering my fairly knock-about existence. I was living in a strange place where I had no roots and no real reason for being there.

I look at photographs from that time and I reel back at how unformed I look: how soft jawed and eager I was, all badly applied make up, badly bleached hair, and insanely inappropriate clothes. But I also look like I'm having a good time. And, for all my reeling about, on the whole I was. New York is full of newcomers and it's not hard to plant yourself in some corner of it pretty snugly. You don't have roots? You lay them down. After a bit I found my place in Cobble Hill, Brooklyn, where I rented the corner of a light-filled parlour floor of

a Brownstone building and furnished it with finds from the flea market. Terence gave me a toaster to celebrate signing my own lease after three years of sub-letting and living in other people's spaces. I didn't use it, but it was there – at least for a bit.

My sister, Bay, arrived and lived in the City, too, and that was wonderful. What's more, I formed my own makeshift family. Nell was not just someone I went to dinner with, but became the person I spoke to, if not saw, every day. I went once a week, almost without fail, to my friends Jackie and Jay's loft for dinner.

Still, I was often tight lipped about what I had been getting up to. One night, in a taxi over the Brooklyn Bridge, on my way to SoHo for dinner, my older sister Rose rang me and told me that her best friend was moving to New York.

'I'm telling you,' she said. 'If one more person moves there I'm going to have to come, too. Everyone I tell everything to is moving to New York.'

'Except for Tom,' I said.

'Except for Tom,' she said. 'Of course, Tom.' Then she paused. 'Who do you tell all your stuff to, Daise?' she asked, her voice filled with concern.

I wondered myself when she asked me that. Good question I thought, and then I thought: no one. I tell my stuff to no one. And I thought, 'Oh God, am I lonely?' I'm a lonely mess.

And then I arrived at Jackie and Jay's and I told them the story, trying to make light of it, as if I were Holly Golightly and the matter was merely something to turn into a monologue, and wasn't it hilarious and preposterous to worry about loneliness and intimacy when we were all having such a thrilling time. And when I'd finished talking, Jay said to me, 'But you tell your stuff to us. That's what we do every week around this table. We tell each other our stuff.'

And so we did, usually accompanied by a wonderful chicken or beef stew, rice and a spinach salad either made by Jackie, without any fuss whatsoever, or bought by her from a Dominican restaurant down the road.

New York beef stew

I was put off stew by the slop served up at boarding school. The only way to eat that stew was to chew each piece of meat interminably until you found a chance to spit it out, secrete it about your person, and then dispose of it. Sometimes there was a dog handy. If you got caught committing this crime, however, you were demoted on the Manners Table, which was posted up every week outside the dining room. Most of us were rated a squirrel. Cats were one better, but the top title, attained only by one or two pupils, was to be crowned a Royal Guest. If you were caught throwing your food underneath the table you became a Caveman immediately, and Cavemen had to sit next to head matron Lucker at every meal for a whole week. Lucker's dog, which bit, was called Bear.

Jackie's stews caused me to re-think, and these days I make them often. This recipe is adapted from one of Daniel Boulud's recipes. Boulud is one of the most revered chefs in New York, and so this stew is in homage to the nights I spent feeling at home in Jackie and Jay's SoHo loft, with its quintessential Manhattan skyline view.

It is a winter stew, to be made when the markets are full of celeriac and parsnips. It also uses horseradish, which, when you cook it, looses its heat and transforms into a mild root vegetable with a soft texture and wonderful flavour.

The secret to any stew is to use really good stewing beef that has been hung for a long time, and to cook everything extremely slowly so that the meat becomes very tender. It is easiest, once you have put everything together in a casserole, to do this in the oven, where the temperature will remain steady.

Important note: I brown the beef in a separate large frying pan, which means that you can do it while the onions and vegetables are sweating in the casserole.

I don't do this primarily for reasons of speed, however, but because invariably some of the beef, flour and oil will burn as you brown it and you don't want to begin your casserole base with bits of black residue. Most books don't warn you about this and so when things get too sizzling you immediately think you must have done something wrong: don't worry, you haven't.

If you find browning quite a lot of spitting meat quite a business, it's not you, it is. Hang in there. Keep your eye on the heat and keep going. It's worth it and is quite enjoyable, as long as no one is watching and you aren't trying to brown too much at once.

Of course, if nothing burns then, once the beef is out, deglaze the frying pan with a slug of wine and pour the juices into the casserole.

Serves 6–8

You will need about 1.35kg of good **stewing beef**, trimmed of fat and cut into 4cm cubes, or thereabouts. Get the vegetables ready: you will need a large **onion** peeled and cut into medium dice, three or four **parsnips** peeled and cut into large chunks and a **celeriac**, also peeled and cut into slightly larger chunks than the parsnips. Peel and grate about 15cm of fresh **horseradish**, so that you end up with about 150g. You will also need three **bay leaves**, twenty **juniper berries**, a large bunch of **fresh dill** and 175ml of **red wine**, 175ml of **vodka**, 50ml of **red wine vinegar**, a tablespoon of **tomato purée** or paste and a small handful of **plain flour**.

Preheat the oven to 150°C/300°F/gas mark 2. Pat the beef with kitchen paper to make sure it is dry; damp meat won't brown. Season the raw beef with salt and freshly ground black pepper and cover it with a light coating of flour. The flour will help thicken the stew as it cooks. Put the coated cubes of beef in a sieve and give it a good shake to get rid of any excess flour.

Heat a tablespoon of olive oil in a large casserole until it is almost smoking and then add the cubes of meat, so that they sizzle as soon as they hit the pan. Do not over-crowd the pan. This is crucial to success. You want the meat to brown on all sides quite quickly, not for it to stew in its own juices, which is what happens if you try to brown too much at once. Once the beef is golden-brown on all sides transfer it to a plate while you cook the vegetables.

Heat another tablespoon of olive oil in a large casserole over a medium heat. Once it is hot, add the onion, juniper berries and a teaspoon of black pepper and cook, stirring, for about six to eight minutes until the onions are translucent. Stir in the red wine vinegar and tomato purée and continue cooking until almost all the liquid has evaporated. Pour in the vodka and red wine and bring to the boil, then add the parsnips and celeriac, bay leaves, dill, 100g of the horseradish and 475ml of water. Now add the beef to the casserole and bring the stew to a steady simmer. Put the lid onto the pot and put it into the oven to braise for two and a half hours.

Use the remaining horseradish to make a horseradish cream by mixing it with about 100ml of crème fraîche (use more or less depending on how strong you like it) and two teaspoons of red wine vinegar (again, keep tasting to determine exact amounts). Season with salt and freshly ground black pepper, and serve with the beef stew, a green salad, and some good crusty bread.

The moment I learnt that cooking could be a pleasure

I loved eating with friends, and yet it didn't occur to me to cook. Ever. The toaster that Terence had bought me was passed on to a friend to make room in the tiny kitchen of my Brooklyn apartment for the things I bought in the Flea Market: pastel-coloured cups and saucers, green plates, the beginnings of an obsessive bowl collection. What was I doing? I was furnishing a life I didn't quite have. But the 'quite' is important. Because I had it sometimes – not in my own apartment using my own teacups – but often at weekends with Nell in Michael's house in Shelter Island, an island which lies between the North and South Forks of Long Island. Michael's Shelter Island house was usually filled with people of all ages, all doing things all together: not only pouring tea out of teapots and eating meals out of nice-looking bowls, but actually making tea, and cooking meals, and taking a good deal of time doing so.

It was in Shelter Island that I realised that cooking was not a chore, but was something that offered all kinds of pleasures. That it was, in short, a way of celebrating being with other people. Another thing that happened during cooking I discovered, was that in-between the chat about how large you should slice potatoes, you quite often told some of the people you were cooking with some of your stuff, without it ever seeming like a big confession. Lastly, and most importantly for me at that time, you didn't even have to actually cook to join in on any of this. It was enough to show willing; to help pick and chop herbs, peel potatoes, dice tomatoes and wash up.

The first time I went to Shelter Island was for a Fourth of July long weekend celebration. Michael had friends over from England and Italy, including Rose Gray and her husband David, and Nell had invited me to join the house party. I remember the weekend in exquisite detail.

I remember feeling entirely happy and occupied all the time. More than that, I can remember how that felt not just in an abstract way. But I don't have to *remember* the actual pleasure to experience it again, because mostly (though not always, certainly not always) this is how I feel whenever I cook now.

The first meal we made that weekend was fish stew. It took six of us five hours to make the stew, but that did include jumping on Michael's sailboat to go and buy fish just as it was being hauled out of the water. It also included breaks. After Rose had cleaned the squid and Dave had gutted the red mullet and bream, Nell made us snacks by grilling sourdough bread, rubbing the toast with a clove of garlic, squishing, hard, a huge cut-open heirloom tomato into each slice, and then generously covering it all with salt and olive oil.

It was the first time I had eaten bruschetta; the first time I had tried Maldon salt; the first time I had tasted sourdough bread. It was also the first time I had dealt with fresh herbs. Rose wanted swathes of them picked from the garden and sent me back when I returned with just a few sprigs. We would need *a lot* of parsley; *loads* of basil; *fistfuls* of thyme and marjoram and oregano and mint. It was also the first time I saw how important good olive oil was in cooking. Before, a bottle of olive oil had sat on my kitchen shelf for months, longer even. That weekend we got through two, brought by Rose from Italy.

Shelter Island fish stew

The fish stew, which we ate around a large square table under a veranda dripping with wisteria and looking directly out to the water, remains the best meal I have ever eaten. Here, found in an old diary filled with invitations and telephone numbers, to-do lists and quotations, self-recriminations and gushes, are my notes on how we, or at least how Rose, with help from all of us, made it.

First gather your ingredients

Peel and chop twelve to fifteen small **new potatoes** into bite-sized pieces. Leave them in a bowl of water while you get on with the rest of the work. You will need about ten good **tomatoes**. Take out their cores, peel and dice them. Reserve the cores for the stock, but throw away the skins. (If it's not summer and the tomatoes aren't good quality use an 800g can of peeled plum tomatoes instead, but not the juices. Sieve to drain them.) Peel ten **garlic** cloves and finely chop eight. Use half a whole large **onion** to make the stock, and use the other half, finely chopped, for the base of the soup. Also chop three carrots for the stock. You will need some **white wine** for both the stock and soup, two fresh **red chillies** left whole and two with their seeds taken out and chopped up small. This stew also uses **fennel seeds**. A lot of fennel seeds. Like about four tablespoons. (Fennel bulbs are also great in the soup base, but since we don't have them, we are using the onion instead.) You need LOTS of **parsley** and **basil**, leaves stripped from their stalks. Also, **mint**, **dill**, about six **peppercorns**, a pinch of **saffron**, some **lemon juice** and a lot of excellent **olive oil**. Only the best will do.

The fish we used was a mixture of a whole **squid**, three **red mullet**, a **bream**, some **mussels** (about a kilo), some **clams** (a bit less than a kilo) and eighteen **langoustines**. (**Turbot** is also excellent in this stew, but it is very expensive. Turbot bones are the best bones for stock and fishmongers will usually give these to you for free if you're buying other fish.) Needless to say, this is a rather extravagant stew.

Now prepare the fish

Start with the squid. Take out the bones and legs from the body. Bones go into the stockpot. Pop out the 'eyes' or 'beads' from the 'flower', as though you are popping out a blackhead. Eyes/beads and guts (cut from tentacles) go into the TRASH.

The body of a squid is a tube and needs to be flattened out. Cut along one half of the tube, so that the body lies flat on the chopping board, then take off the wings. (These go into the stock, as they are too tough for the soup.) Also scrape off all the gungy stuff from inside the now flattened body. The gunge goes in the trash. Chop up the, by now, tasty-looking body into largish bite-sized pieces. You can ask the fishmonger to do all of this, except the final chopping, which is not a bad idea.

Fillet the red mullet and bream (or get your fishmonger to do it for you) and cut into generous bite-sized chunks. Add the fish bones and heads to the stockpot.

Now for the shellfish. Wash the mussels well in the sink. If any of them are open or have broken shells throw them out. Do the same with the clams.

Steam the mussels and clams by putting the mussels first, then the clams, into a large saucepan with a lid. Add a lot of olive oil (half a glass full), a whole red chilli and a small glass of white wine. Put the lid on and turn the heat to high. Shake the pan often.

In five minutes the shells will have opened and the mussels and clams will be ready. Any that are still closed, chuck. When the shellfish is cold enough to touch, take some of the mussels and clams out of their shells. Keep some in – about half and half. Strain the juices from the pan into stockpot.

The langoustines are fine as they are; you peel them when you eat them.

Next, make the stock

Into the stockpot with all the fish 'extras' (the squid wings, fish bones and heads, the shellfish liquid and the turbot bones, if you're using them) add the tomato cores, the two whole garlic cloves, half the onion, the three carrots, one whole red chilli NOT chopped up, some parsley and basil and their stalks, mint, dill and the peppercorns. Add equal amounts of cold water and white wine, so that everything is just covered. Bring to the boil and then skim off the white scum that forms.

Once the stock is boiling, lower the heat to a simmer. Fish stock needs to cook for just TWENTY MINUTES. No longer; it's not necessary.

To make the soup base

While the stock is cooking, start on the soup base. You will need another big pot for this. Over a medium heat, heat about half as much olive oil as went into the mussels. Add the two chopped chillies and the fennel seeds, then the chopped onion. After the onion, add the rest of the chopped garlic, some more parsley, chopped, basil and dill.

Pour in a large slug of white wine – about half a glass. Cook for about five minutes and stir. Add the chopped tomatoes and cook everything over a gentle heat for about forty-five minutes. Keep tasting it. Add salt and freshly ground black pepper, to taste. Add more chilli if you think it needs it. (Ours didn't.)

While this is bubbling away, boil the chopped potatoes in salty water until they are nearly, but not quite, done. Drain and let them cool.

Combine the fish, stock and soup

The base of your soup should still be cooking away on its gentle heat.

Add the fish stock to it and bring this stock-enhanced soup up to the boil. Add the bream and red mullet and bring back to the boil. Then add the squid. Bring back to the boil again.

Take off the heat and gently stir in the potatoes and all the shellfish, including the langoustines. Season with the herbs and a pinch of saffron.

Finalement, add more, yes, more olive oil and a squeeze or two of lemon juice.

When we finished the fish stew we went for an icy swim in a nearby lake and then Michael took us to the mainland in his boat, so that we could watch the firework displays lying flat on our backs on the playing fields of the local high school. We felt full and pleased with ourselves. By the time we got home, however, we were peckish. Adam, one of the guests at the house who had once worked at The River Café before moving to Italy, made us supper. It was perfect.

The perfect supper for after a very large, late lunch

Cut in half as many **avocados** as there are people to serve, and scoop out their stones using a teaspoon. The avocados must be perfectly ripe. Generously sprinkle **Maldon salt** into the empty pool of each half. Add a good squeeze of **lime juice**. Fill up the pool with very good **olive oil**. Now eat.

Just in case my Fourth of July weekend in Shelter Island was not magical enough, I left it on a tiny plane bound for Martha's Vineyard and a new lover. The lover and I had only just met. He was older than me and had a daughter and a career in the movies. The day after we'd met and fallen in love (or so I'd thought), he jumped on a plane to Los Angeles and I had thought: perhaps, then, that is that. But he had called me while I was in Shelter Island and, because he had rented a house on Martha's Vineyard, he suggested we meet there as soon as possible. When I asked how to get there he said he'd send a plane. I thought: Not bad or what?

Only it did get bad and it got bad quickly. The day I arrived I made the bruschetta I had loved so much in Shelter Island. We bought heirloom tomatoes, garlic, good bread, salt and olive oil at the farm stand on the way back from the airport. His best friend was staying at the house, too, only no one, except me, ate the bruschetta. The two men weren't interested. They drank beer. We were going to have pizza later with friends, they said.

The friends were glamorous, sophisticated, well-groomed women who dropped by the house all the time. They wore tiny white tennis shorts or perfect jeans and T-shirts that hung off their bony frames. On their feet they wore Tod's driving shoes and on their hands they wore chunky gold rings and they laughed about island gossip and jumped in and out of their open-top cars, having just come from drinks with Carly Simon or thrashing each other on the tennis court. I didn't drive. I didn't have any gossip. I couldn't play tennis. I wore brightly coloured bras and revealing summer dresses and strappy, shiny shoes from the flea market. I was bigger than everyone else, fatter, younger, my hair was a mess, and I wasn't successful. I wrote tiny articles about up-and-coming actresses or pop stars for glossy magazines. The women dropping by had written novels or produced movies or had television shows. One was a member of a rock band and was married to a movie star. We went to their house for dinner and everybody took turns singing rock songs. I can't sing.

Plus it turned out my lover drank a lot. He got up in the middle of the night to drink, say, sixteen or seventeen cans of beer, before returning upstairs. He drank in the day, too. And all of us smoked pot. Only no one thought to throw away their beer cans or empty an ashtray or pick anything up from the floor except me, and so we lived in a pigsty. And so it went on, until I got myself home.

I didn't make bruschetta when I got back to my apartment in Brooklyn, and the fish stew recipe remained unused, until relatively recently, in my diary. When a friend from London came to stay and offered one night to cook for me, I was amazed.

'Cook here? In this tiny kitchen? Alone?' I said.

'Yes,' Jim said. 'How did I usually do it?'

'I don't,' I told him. But indeed when I got home from work there was a meal waiting for me.

Jim had cooked two slabs of steak, and to go with it, no sauce or vegetables, but a lot of plain pasta.

It wasn't a very good meal, but that didn't matter. He neither made excuses nor expected praise. He had cooked so that we could sit down and eat and talk, drink some wine, relax and be still. What was the big deal?

Cooking very plainly is of course the way most of us try to cook these days. It means you are reliant on your ingredients for flavour, rather than a cloaking sauce. It is hard to beat a piece of very fresh fish plainly cooked with some boiled potatoes and a green salad – except if you add a salsa verde. Salsa verde was another of the things I learnt about during that Fourth of July weekend on Shelter Island. Now, in the summer, I make a bowl of it most days and put it on the table along with the salt and pepper and water jug.

Salsa verde

I make my salsa verde with a lot of herbs – mostly parsley and basil, and a little less mint (unless I'm making it specifically to go with lamb, in which case I increase the mint factor and lower the basil significantly, if not omit it completely). But my salsa verde recipe varies a little every time

I make it, depending on the strength and taste of the herbs, which varies depending on how much sunshine they get, and how fresh or strong or mild the garlic is, which varies depending on the time of year. In spring, for example, I use more of it than I do in the autumn.

One of the pleasures of this sauce is tasting it as you go along and making adjustments, which also means that you learn how salt or mustard or garlic or capers or vinegar can alter flavour.

When I spent a day teaching Bay how to cook, one of the first things we made was a salsa verde for this very reason – and of course because it is so versatile and delicious and transforming. If you buy a piece of fish and grill it and boil some new potatoes you will have a good supper, but if you add salsa verde, you will lift the whole meal a very big notch.

You can find salsa verde recipes just about anywhere, and once you start making it you will develop your own according to your personal tastes. Here is a general guide to mine:

Take the leaves off one large bunch of basil, one large bunch of **parsley** and a much smaller bunch (about a third as big) of **mint**. In a food processor place two cloves of **garlic**, two tablespoons of **capers**, six salted **anchovies** (rinsed well to get rid of some of the salt and with their flesh gently peeled away from their spines), two teaspoons of **Dijon mustard**, two tablespoons of **red wine vinegar** and the leaves from all the herbs.

While the food processor is running, pour in some good extra virgin **olive oil** in a steady medium-fast stream (if you go too slowly everything will be pulsed into oblivion and you want the salsa to have an interesting and coarse texture). Keep pouring until the sauce is bound together – this will take about five or six tablespoons of oil. Taste and add a little **Maldon salt** if you think it needs it (use great restraint with the salt until you've tasted the salsa; the ingredients you have used are all salty themselves) and some freshly ground **black pepper**, then taste again and make adjustments.

Remember you can always add more herbs and oil if you've over done the garlic or mustard or anchovies.

For pudding Jim had bought sliced mangoes from the delicatessen around the corner. I knew that mango well. I bought it, along with a cup of coffee and sometimes a bagel, and ate it everyday for breakfast. Sometimes I would tear open the packaging and eat mouthfuls of the fruit on my way home. Inevitably, I was caught doing this by someone I had once dated.

'Hey there!' the ex said.

'Hey!' I said back, my mouth full of mango. He looked down at the polystyrene platter with its torn plastic wrapping and got-at remains.

'You actually buy that stuff?' he said, both amused and disgusted.

'Yeah,' I said. Was he always so anal? 'I even eat it.'

'So I see,' he replied lightly. I could tell that he was running over our sexual history in his head. Yes, I wanted to say to him, you really did have sex with me.

'Think how many hands have touched that fruit,' he continued. 'Think of the guy who prepared it. Don't you wonder where his hands have been? And you're eating it, straight from the packet?'

'How else would I eat it?' I asked.

'Apart from putting it in a bowl first.'

'*You would wash it first,*' he said incredulously. 'You would wash it *before* putting it in a bowl, *before* putting it into your body.'

I didn't know what to say to that, and though he didn't persuade me to despise the mango, I *was* embarrassed by my greed. I slunk away and hoped that if I ever ran into him again I would be at least twenty pounds lighter. That would teach him.

Eight years later I no longer buy pre-cut mango. I buy them by the box in summer when the Alphonsos arrive in the Middle Eastern grocery shops and, as well as eating them plain, I make mango sorbet. I have made many sorbets over the last few years, but the ones I am asked for over and over again are mango and strawberry. Now I want to run into that good-looking, hygiene-obsessed guy.

'Remember me?' I'd say. 'The slut who ate dirty mango? I make mango sorbet now. What do you say to that?'

But he is probably married to a beautiful model and they probably live off mango martinis and he'd probably shrug and say, 'Oh. Great. Glad to see you've done something with your life.'

Mango sorbet

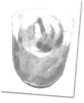

I don't know where I found this recipe, but it works like magic as long as you have really good ripe mangoes. If you can't get them don't make the sorbet.

Serves 6–8

4 fantastic mangoes, preferably the small Alphonso mangoes that you get in summer (in which case use five)

juice of a lime

85g of sugar

6 tbsp glucose (you can get glucose in health food shops if you can't find it at your supermarket, which I never can)

2 free-range egg whites

1 Peel, chop and stone the mangoes, and put the chunks into the food processor with the lime juice, sugar and glucose. Blitz this mixture together until it forms a smooth purée, adding a little water if you think it needs loosening up.

2 Put your purée in a saucepan and bring it to the boil. As soon as it has boiled, take it off the heat and let it cool.

3 Meanwhile, whisk the egg whites until they are just frothy and fold them into the cooled purée. Put the mixture in the fridge for half an hour to chill.

4 Once chilled, pour into an ice cream maker and churn until frozen. Decant into a container with a tight-fitting lid and freeze for three hours. If you freeze it for longer, make sure you take it out half an hour before serving it, so that it is soft enough to eat.

Strawberry sorbet

adapted from *The River Café Cook Book*
by Rose Gray and Ruth Rogers

Unlike the mango sorbet, this one doesn't need the best, sweetest fruit (God knows the recipe uses enough sugar. God knows it's worth it), so it's a fantastic thing to make if there hasn't been enough sunshine and the berries are limping in at half-mast.

Serves 6–8

2 lemons
400-450g of caster sugar
(depending on how sweet
your strawberries are)
900g strawberries, hulled

1 Put one whole lemon, skin and all, into the food processor, and blitz with the sugar.

2 Add the strawberries and blend the mixture together, then push it all through a sieve. This takes a bit of effort, but keep going.

3 Add the juice from about half a lemon to the, by now, beautiful mixture, and taste. The flavour of the lemon should be intense but should not overpower the strawbugs. Add more lemon juice if you think it needs it.

4 Chill the mixture in the fridge for half an hour, then pour into an ice cream maker and churn until frozen. Decant into a container with a tight fitting lid and freeze for three hours. If you freeze it for longer make sure you take it out half an hour before serving it, so it is soft enough to eat.

Johnny, jaundice and the lentil stew

I met Johnny in an East Village nightclub where he was performing a drag act. I was with a friend who knew him, and we sat watching him on a banquette next to his sleeping white Bull Terrier, Ruby. When he came to join us, I told him that I'd grown up with a white Bull Terrier called Mona.

'No?' he said. 'How *fabulous*. Don't you *j'adore* Bull Terriers?'

Johnny taught the fashion crowd to say 'I *j'adore*'. It's just one of his gifts to the world.

He is a Buddhist, and he lives in a tiny apartment painted purple with red-and-white gingham curtains, and, in one corner, taking up a good deal of space, an altar where he chants every day. As well as being a sometime drag queen ('draggage') Johnny is a photographer. He discovered Buddhism when he photographed Tina Turner in the early '80s.

'You are *incredible*,' he said to her. 'I'm *j'adoring* your energy. What's your secret darling?'

'I chant,' she told him, and that was it.

Ruby died a long time ago, but Johnny now lives with two Hairless Chinese Crested dogs called Hobson and Gypsy, and a demanding Poohuahua (all four pounds of her) called Stella.

Johnny has long hair with a fringe, and huge, square glasses. He makes friends all the time – down the street, with waiters, in shops, at parties, at the park, wherever. He calls the young friends he makes through Buddhism his soldiers, and he is never without one or two nearby, helping him with his computer or photography or a layout, or some other errand or chore. I'm not a soldier, although I'm sure I began as one. Instead, early on in our relationship we began to call each other Mum. He calls other people Mum, too. But then, so do I.

'Hi Mum,' he'd ring up and say.

'Hi Mum,' I'd reply, 'How're you?'

'Heinous,' he'd say. 'Tragic.' And we'd talk about a job going wrong, or a man not returning a call. We once spotted a Keanu Reeves look-alike in a health food restaurant on Madison Avenue, next to the old *Vogue* offices, where I used to work. He was eating alone and so we sat down next to him, found out that his name was Ezra, forced him to make friends with us, and competed with each other trying to lure him into bed. But Ezra abstained from many things: drinking, fruit on anything other than a completely empty stomach, fun it seemed; certainly sex with either of us.

'Fucking Ezra,' Johnny would say, getting bored with his blank refusal to be seduced. 'How heinous is he? I've had enough, Mum.'

Sometimes Johnny and I talked about some ailment or other. Johnny is often not in great health, though he never complains. Things go wrong with his eyes and one of his feet fairly regularly, and he once came a real cropper with both jaundice and pancreatitis. He turned yellow and had to be rushed to hospital, where he and all of us – his friends and sisters and soldiers – were told that he would die.

Only of course he didn't.

'Die of jaundice?' he said when he came round. 'No, I don't think so. Not today darling.'

Naturally enough, Johnny and I both fancied one of his doctors. We didn't get anywhere with him either,

but we'd talk about him every night when Johnny was allowed out of the hospital, and I moved into his tiny apartment as an on-call soldier for a few days. We slept in the same bed and watched old movies in the middle of the night on AMC.

'What's AMC?' I asked on the first night.

'American Movie Classics,' Johnny said, outraged. 'What else don't you know?'

We didn't sleep much. It was crowded in the bed between me, Johnny and Belle, the Bull Terrier he had inherited after Ruby died. He had an unbelievably thick and suffocating duvet that sucked out any available oxygen in the room, and there wasn't much, what with the windows shut, Bette Davis shouting, and us farting all night. We farted because Johnny's sister, Eve, had made a giant pot of lentil stew intended to feed us for days – which it did; we lived on it. In the mornings I'd go out and get bagels or muffins and coffee, but otherwise it was lentils all the way. Sometimes Johnny made smoothies, but they weren't a million miles away from the stew either.

'Do you still put nuts and seeds in your smoothies?' I asked him out of the blue – a total non-sequitor – in an email I sent him recently. He replied immediately.

'Well, I start with a banana,' his email went. 'Then apple juice, blueberries, raspberries, strawbs, half a spoon of wheat germ and either some flax seeds or walnuts for that crunch factor you hate.'

I've never had lentil stew since those happy, slobby, bed-bound days with Johnny, but I do eat lentils a lot, often for lunch when I am alone, with little else except a bit of feta cheese, olive oil, vinegar and parsley, plus whatever bonus vegetables or strip of ham I might have at hand.

A lentil lunch
I use red lentils for making dhal or pumpkin soup and green lentils for sprouting, but I use Puy lentils from France or Castelluccio lentils from Italy when I'm eating them like this, because they are the most delicious.

Put a couple of handfuls of **lentils** into a large-ish saucepan of cold water with the sort of vegetables you'd use for making stock. Cold water is important because it brings out the flavours of what's in the pot as it heats up. I usually put in a stick of **celery**, a peeled or cleaned **carrot** or two, snapped in half, some **parsley** stalks (keep the leaves for later), an **onion**, peeled and quartered, a **bay leaf**, and some **garlic**. If I'm doing a lot of lentils then I'll slice a whole head of garlic in half horizontally and put that in, or if I'm making less or I'm a bit short, I'll put in a couple of peeled cloves. Don't worry if you don't have all these things. You can always just boil the lentils in plain water and nothing else, or else add just one or two of the veg. Bring the water to the boil, then turn the heat down and let it simmer for about twenty minutes.

Taste a lentil or two to see if they're done. They should retain a bit of bite. It's better not to over cook the lentils, but they are not too ill-humoured if the worst comes to the worst. Drain them immediately they are done, and discard the veg. It has done its work.

Put the lentils into a bowl and dress at once with **Maldon salt**, freshly ground **black pepper** and one part **sherry vinegar** to three parts good olive oil. Be very generous with the dressing, as the lentils will drink it up.

Chop up a big handful of **parsley** and, if you've got it, plenty of fresh **marjoram**, and put that in, too, along with a few chopped **spring onions** or half a really finely sliced **red onion**.

Dressed lentils like this are very good served with anything, be it meat or fish. (If they are accompanying something elaborate, leave out the onions, or just dress them in oil and lemon juice, salt and pepper. You don't want to over-accessorise.)

To turn these already delicious lentils into a fantastic one-bowl lunch, add whatever takes your fancy. My favourite combination is a bit of **feta cheese** crumbled in, some roasted or boiled **beetroot**, chopped up, and a torn piece or two of **prosciutto**. But **cherry tomatoes** cut in half, or bigger tomatoes diced up are delicious; so are chunks of **cucumber**; so is roasted **squash**, or pumpkin.

Another very good thing to do is to mix in strips or small chunks of **pancetta** or **bacon** with a handful of baby **spinach**, which, if you add it when the lentils are still quite hot, will wilt perfectly.

A lentil and fish supper

For spicier lentils, cook the **lentils** as above, but dress them with **oil**, **red wine vinegar**, chopped **spring onions**, **salt** and **pepper**. Add a finely chopped **green chilli**, a teaspoon each of **ground coriander** and **ground cumin** and a handful of **fresh coriander leaves**.

This is particularly good when served with fish – a fillet of **sea bass** each, say, brushed on both sides with **olive oil** and cooked on an extremely hot griddle pan, skin-side down. Season the fillets with **Maldon salt** and freshly ground **black pepper** while they are cooking and after about three minutes turn them over and cook the other side for another two, or until the fish is just cooked through. Serve with a wedge of lime.

Johnny was also a friend of Nell and Eamon's, and he, too, sometimes came to Shelter Island. One weekend he arrived and immediately came down with flu. He lay, cheery enough, on the sofa all weekend in a pair of leopard-print pyjamas watching Stanley Kubrick's *Barry Lyndon*. We bustled about around him. A friend of Nell's, a set-designer called Bob, was also staying, and an art critic who had a house on the island came over for supper.

It was spring and the first of the asparagus had arrived, and so to begin the meal we bought an extravagant amount of it from the farm stand. Nell and Eamon made a Hollandaise sauce, and we spent a good deal of time laying the table to celebrate our feast.

The asparagus was served on an enormous and beautiful platter that sat in the middle of the table, with another bowl for the Hollandaise, so that we could continue to pick at it while we talked and drank.

The art critic told us about growing up in a family of lawyers and being sent to a Jesuit boarding school in a place far away from any art. He talked about one day seeing a postcard one of his schoolmasters had been sent, which he had pinned to his door. The postcard was of a painting by Georgio de Chirico and the art critic, then a child, was struck by its beauty and complexity, and that

was how he had discovered art and pursued his calling. He told this story with great skill, as if he himself were painting a picture in front of us.

He talked about learning and childhood and suffering and isolation and the joy of discovery and the relief in finding that there were footholds and guy ropes and signposts to help you navigate being human if you just looked at the way others tried to explain what they saw and felt and experienced.

He spoke intimately and with great fluency, and when he had finished talking he found that the cigarette he had lit had burned down to his fingers, and not looking for an ashtray, not even for a moment, he stubbed it out on the platter in the middle of the table in the remains of Nell's Hollandaise.

Asparagus

Asparagus is easy. The only rule is when to cook it and that is when it is growing somewhere near you, which in England is very late April or early May.

Using a sharp knife, chop off the bottom woody part of each asparagus spear (about 3 or 4 cm), then peel the bottom third of the trimmed stalks using a vegetable peeler. You don't have to do this, but I always do, as it looks even more enticing this way and gets rid of some of the coarser peel. It doesn't take long and, anyway, it's asparagus – one of the jewels of the vegetable garden. What wouldn't you do for asparagus?

Then you simply boil or steam the asparagus. I usually boil it, using an oval casserole dish, large enough so that the asparagus fit in easily. You don't have to use much water – enough to cover it and then a bit more – but make sure it is salted and boiling when you put the asparagus in. It will take about five minutes to cook – the bottom of the stalk should be just tender. Check using the tip of a knife, or better yet by tasting a spear.

Hollandaise

I was scared of making Hollandaise, though for no rational reason. I'd never tried making it until my friend Rory O'Connell showed me how to do it. Classic Hollandaise is made with a reduction of white wine and shallot, but this recipe uses just two egg yolks (freeze the whites to use for another time – maybe a mango sorbet?), 110g butter, which should be salted (keep it cold and cut it into smallish chunks) and a squeeze of lemon juice, as well as a little water. It is delicious. The secret, of course, lies in the quality of the eggs and butter that you use.

Put two **egg yolks** into a small, heavy saucepan with low sides and a thick bottom. Add a dessertspoon of water and whisk together thoroughly. Now put the saucepan over a low heat. If you turn the heat up too high the eggs will simply scramble. Add the **butter** a few pieces – about three or four – at a time and *keep whisking*. As soon as the cubes you have added have melted, add a few more. Gradually this mixture will begin to look like a sauce and thicken up a little.

141

Be very careful with the heat. It's a good idea, especially the first few times you make Hollandaise, to keep a jug of cold water on hand. If the sauce looks like it is beginning to scramble or curdle, get it off the heat, add a dessertspoon of the water and whisk it in. You are whisking all the time anyway.

When all the butter has been whisked in, add a squeeze of **lemon juice** (about a dessertspoon) and taste. The sauce should now be of a light coating consistency.

Remember: Hollandaise is served warm, not hot. You have to keep it warm, therefore, without ever reheating it, which, being an egg-based sauce, it doesn't like. Keep it in a bowl on the shelf above your cooker, in a pan of barely simmering water or on the coolest surface of an Aga, if you have one. Or pour it into a warm thermos flask. If it forms a skin in its bowl just whisk it in immediately before serving.

Here is a gift I received from my friend Bess. It is her recipe for ham cooked in cola, which she makes every year as part of the Thanksgiving feast she gives in East Hampton, and for which she is justly famous.

I met Bess when I started to work full-time for American *Vogue*. She was a senior editor and writer there. My job was as a writer on the beauty desk and my immediate boss was a beautiful woman called Amy Astley. Amy caught the subway to work everyday in high heels. But they weren't high enough, she explained, and so, when she arrived at her desk, she swapped her high heels for higher ones. Everyone wore high heels in the office. They wore them mostly with pale brown Helmet Lang trousers and a slim fitting cashmere sweater or a crisp shirt and a tailored jacket.

I wore long denim skirts and sequinned tops and didn't know how a magazine worked or how to write a story. No one seemed to mind. Instead, Amy and Bess and an editor called Charles, who was the reason I got a job at *Vogue* in the first place, taught me, or began to teach me how to be a journalist. No one minded what I wore either. Everyone else looked smart as pins and I didn't and that was fine. You will see how lucky I was to work with Bess by her recipe.

Bess's Hatfield ham

First of all, you have to make sure you get exactly the right kind of ham. You do NOT want what's called a 'country ham' (which is hard-cured and needs to be soaked for hours to get the salt out, and has a hard, prosciutto-like texture). You do NOT want some honey ham abomination. You need, specifically, a genuine, whole Hatfield ham from Pennsylvania, which is salt and smoke-cured, with the bone still in it. It's salty and hickory-smokey. I buy Hatfield ham from the IGA supermarket in Bridgehampton, NY, which also carries certain other pork products, because there is a fair-sized African-American population in Bridgehampton that knows hams from hams.

Technically, one of these hams is like a hot dog, it is already cooked and cured; though you certainly wouldn't want to gnaw a bite out of the unbaked hock. So what you do when you bake it is flavour it with a glaze, give it a dark crust, and dry it out a bit by putting it in a moderate oven for an hour and a half or so.

(To interrupt Bess for a moment: you can't buy a Hatfield ham in the UK, but that's okay. In America they call all cured legs of pork – cooked or uncooked – ham, whereas here, uncooked ham is called gammon. Therefore, what you want to buy is a piece of gammon, which will have been cured by your butcher. You can buy it either smoked or unsmoked. Bess recommends a smoky ham, but try out both because it's a matter of taste. Smoked gammon is cold smoked – it's not like smoked salmon, for example: you can't eat it.

Bess insists her ham be on the bone, and indeed if you are cooking for many this is an ideal way to do it. You may have to order it on the bone in advance from your butcher, as most don't stock such large pieces of gammon on a day-to-day basis.

But, at the risk of Bess's wrath, I frequently cook smaller pieces of gammon off the bone using her recipe, adjusting her amounts accordingly. It all goes swimmingly.

Gammon, because it is cured, is usually overly salty. It's a good idea, therefore, to soak it in a large pot of cold water for 24 hours prior to cooking it. Another way to de-salt it is to put it in a saucepan of cold water, bring the water briefly to the boil, then strain the gammon. (Some gammons are so mildly cured that they don't need this step.) One other thing that Bess doesn't do to her Hatfield ham, but that I recommend with gammon, is to peel off its rind before scoring the fat and slapping on the glaze. The rind is simply too tough to eat.)

The glaze (for a 3kg Hatfield ham)

Yes, I use **cola**. I take a large bowl, and dump 400g of moist, dark-brown **Muscovado sugar** into it. Then I take a 400g jar of **black molasses** and pour most of it over the sugar. Black molasses is from sugar cane; NOT from beets; it is NOT treacle. NO. Look for 'blackstrap' molasses.

Then add a large amount of **mustard powder**, say, three tablespoons, two tablespoons of **Dijon mustard**, four tablespoons of dried **ginger** and a good tablespoon or two of ground **nutmeg**. I take a wooden spoon and mix it up. Then I take an **orange**, split it in two, and squeeze the juice over the mix. Then I rip a bit of the flesh out of the orange, the pulp, toss it in and stir it around. If I have some orange juice, I'll add 80–100ml of that, too. And then I pour over about $2/3$ of a can of cola.

The cola starts to foam. 'Whoa,' I say, and stir it around. It should be paste-like and thicker than cake batter. If it is too liquidy, toss in some more of the brown sugar and other dry ingredients until it's nice and spicy and not too runny.

Prepare the ham

Some people cut off all the fat, but I don't. I might trim off a few really fatty parts if there are any, but I leave most of it alone. Then, take a large, sharp knife, and score the fatty side of the ham with a bold diamond pattern, hashing crossways through the fat and down into a bit of the skin, around 5mm deep (although it's totally fine if it goes a bit deeper through the fattier bits).

Put the ham scored-side up in a roasting pan. A snug fit is fine, you don't want a gigantic pan that will dissipate the juices and glaze. Pour a large amount of glaze over the top of the ham and spread it out; and feel a bit sad when it slides off the top of the ham. But don't worry! It's okay! (You will still have a huge quantity of extra glaze in your big bowl. You will even have some leftover at the end. There is no use for it. It's wasteful, I'm afraid, but it goes in the trash.) Pour more cola into the bottom of the pan; maybe another $^2/_3$ of a can.

Bake the ham
Preheat the oven to 170°C/325°F/gas mark 3. Place the glazed ham in its tray in the oven, uncovered. After half an hour, add some more glaze, just by 'globbing' it onto the top of the ham. Add more glaze twice during baking.

When the ham has a thick, dark, delicious crust of molasses goodness, which will take 1 $^1/_2$–2 hours, the ham is done. Boost up the oven if it doesn't look dark and crusty enough.

People will cry out, 'My Lord, how White Trash to put cola on your pristine ham! Why don't you braise it, instead? Aren't you desecrating that ham?'

And you will say, 'I do it because when you taste it you will see that this is the most delicious ham in the world.'

When I stayed with Bess for Thanksgiving everyone pitched in, and many had their own specialties that they cooked and added to the feast. Except for me. I loved being in the kitchen and being set to work, but cook? No. I didn't cook. It took being cast off into the middle of the ocean to make me take hold of a saucepan, turn on an oven, and say: I am not here by chance or at the behest of someone else, and I will not sing for my supper to repay such luck: I'll cook.

If I were spending Thanksgiving with Bess this year, I'd cook a pudding that would be up to following Bess's magnificent Hatfield ham, and that pudding would have to be an apple one, just as at Christmas it must be plum. And the apple pudding I would make would be French, because American apple puddings (apple crisp and apple crumb and apple muffins) tend to involve distracting things like acres of oat flakes. And that French apple pudding could only be, on a late November evening, Tarte Tatin.

Learning to make Tarte Tatin: the pre-lesson

There was one lesson I learnt quickly when I arrived off the boat in London and began to branch away from rice and cabbage salads, roast chicken and pasta, and that lesson was: some things you only learn through practice.

When people talk about a seasoned cook, they are saying something significant. However much you read, however many questions you ask, however much you watch and hover over a cook like I did with Bess in East Hampton or Nell and Rose in Shelter Island, and however many recipes you follow, some things can only be mastered by practice; by getting to know well, how, say, sugar responds to heat, or flour and water to yeast, or pastry to the heat of your hands. Then, of course, there is how things taste: the transforming effect of salt being just one lesson that you learn the more you cook.

When I arrived back in London I was excited to cook. I would no longer be in a galley kitchen with limited pots and pans and tools and very few recipes, but in London and Somerset with potentially untold

resources. What wouldn't I master? Well, Tarte Tatin for a start. Or at least not at the first attempt. Or the second. Or the third.

No one says that your first Tarte Tatin won't work very well and nor, for that matter, will your first four soda breads or your first pizza or your first jelly. But *I* know. They won't. I followed detailed instructions to the letter and still my tart fell out of its pan in pieces, and it did this more than once.

I wasn't doing anything wrong specifically: there was no light-switch moment – no 'Aha! I see I've been using the wrong flour all this time' realisation – it's just that it takes practice and practice only (though the right pan does help) to know how long to cook the sugar before adding the apples and how long to cook the apples before adding the pastry.

Most people who cook learn gradually, as they grow up, with the activity turning up a gear when something happens in their life – they start a family or fall in love or live and eat regularly with flatmates. Curiosity helps and so does greed and so does doggedness and so, of course, does a sense of taste. But, mostly, it is down to practice. Some people might make their first botched Tarte Tatin, watched over by their grandmother (though do they? What in fact do they do?) and then proceed from there, over the years, to achieve perfection.

Not me. I made one a day for about a week, such was my weird obsession in wanting to get it right. Also, I had just returned to London from America. I had spent two months on a boat in a community; I hadn't been alone for a moment. Now I was a freelance writer just settling into an ostensibly new city. Where were my merry men? Who was I supposed to eat with and cook for every day? I wasn't sure. But I was sure that one of the things I would be cooking would be a Tarte Tatin that came out of its tin all of a beautiful caramelised magnificent piece.

You can find a recipe for Tarte Tatin in a million different books. I tried many of them. I had my first success using the recipe in *Sally Clarke's Book*. It is not that her recipe is different from anybody else's that makes it so useful, it's the way that she describes the technique. Classic

Tarte Tatin, which hers is, is just that: a classic, un-mucked-about recipe as invented, by accident so the story goes, in 1889 by Stephanie and Caroline Tatin at their hotel, Hotel Tatin, in North-Central France.

I follow Sally Clarke to the letter, and so reproduce her recipe and description exactly.

Sally Clarke's Tarte Tatin
from *Sally Clarke's Book* by Sally Clarke

The other thing I did on my quest, which was a big help, was to buy a special Tarte Tatin pan. It's the right size and shape (about 24cm across for this recipe), has handles in the right place, and a non-stick coating. Mine cost about £25.00 and was absolutely worth it. Otherwise you will need a clean, heavy based sauté pan with an ovenproof handle.

Serves 6

For the pastry	*For the tarte*
120g flour	150g butter, soft but not oily
pinch of salt	125g sugar
60g butter, chilled and diced	2kg firm eating apples
40g sugar	(do not use cooking
1 tbsp water	apples as they collapse
1 egg yolk	down too much)

The pastry

1 Sieve the flour and salt into a bowl and rub in the butter until it resembles fine breadcrumbs.

2 Stir in the sugar and add the water and egg yolk, mixing gently until the mixture comes together. Gently knead for a few moments until it looks smooth. Wrap and chill for at least one hour.

The tarte

1 Using your fingertips spread the butter over the surface of the pan like a paste, as evenly as possible. Sprinkle over the sugar as evenly as possible and leave in a cool place.

2 Peel the apples whole, cut in half from top to bottom and remove the cores carefully. Do not worry if the apples discolour.

3 Place the apple halves around the inside rim of the pan, standing them upright, stalk end up, gently pressing them into the butter and sugar to keep them firmly in place. Make sure they are intersecting. The result must be a very tightly fitted pan of apples without any space to move.

4 Roll out the pastry to approx 3cm wider than the diameter of the pan and leave in a cold place.

5 Preheat the oven to 200°C/400°F/gas mark 6.

6 Place the pan over a high heat and cook the apples until the butter and sugar begin to caramelise and the apples start to soften. Turn down the heat a little if the apples start to burn before softening, and increase it if there seems to be a lack of colour to the apples and too much juice overflowing from the pan covering the cooker in a sticky caramel. The trick here is to start caramelising the apples whilst at the same time evaporating off some of the excess juices as the fruit starts to soften. From time to time turn an apple half towards the centre of the pan to check the amount of colour on the base. Once the majority of the apples are a medium gold the tart is ready for the oven.

7 Remove the pan from the heat and cover the apples with the pre-rolled pastry. Tuck the excess pastry around the edge down in between the apples and the pan. Make one large incision in the centre to allow the steam to escape during the cooking, place it on a baking sheet to catch the drips, and then put it in the oven.

8 Bake for about twenty minutes, until the pastry is crisp and golden.

9 Remove from the oven and place a serving dish upside-down over the pan. Invert, allowing all the juices from the pan to arrive on the plate with the tart. Eat as soon as possible with lots of crème fraîche.

Chapter five
Returning home.
Cooking for one or
fourteen, and the
dangers of bravado

Louche ways and tofu in the USA

'Why did you come back?' And 'Do you miss it?' These were the questions I was asked most often when I returned to London after nearly eight years in New York. I didn't know the answer to either question. For one thing, I hadn't planned to go to America in the first place, and didn't know if I would stay 'back' and, for another, I'd never made a decision about what to do with my life, and didn't know how to start. Becoming a journalist, for instance, and living in New York had happened almost by accident. I met an editor of American *Vogue* by chance after I spent a summer in Long Island tutoring an English 17-year-old for the 'A' levels he would take at boarding school in England the following year.

'What do you do?' the editor asked me. He was called Charles.

'I'm a tutor,' I said. 'Temporarily. To earn money. But what I want to do is write. Really, I'm a writer,' I heard myself pronounce.

'Oh,' said Charles. 'A *writer*. How very grand. And what have you written?' He said the last word as if it began with an 'h'.

The truth was that I hadn't written anything – except for a short piece about my mother, Polly Devlin, herself a real writer, for a regular unknown-person-writes-about-being-related-to-person-of-interest slot in the Irish Sunday Tribune. What I had done, apart from spending the summer teaching, was bum around bits of the US, either by myself or with my American friend Kyle.

('Let's see what happens,' I had faxed Kyle before the trip – this was in the days before email. 'My priorities include listening to as much good music, preferably live, as possible, and getting laid a lot.' Obviously, I left the fax by the machine for my dad to find.)

We had driven her mother's 1972 open-top Buick Skylark from Santa Fe to San Francisco, and had various adventures along the way: taking magic mushrooms in Utah's Canyonlands, sleeping on the beach in Puerto Rico (a minor detour), drinking a lot of beer in hot tubs after pretending to rock climb and mountain bike in California, and gambling in Nevada. I had also spent some time bumming around Miami Beach with a bass player and his band mates, and hanging out at music festivals around New Orleans.

Kyle was – and is – a fantastic cook; she grew up in New Mexico, and most people who grow up there are. They travel with things like green chillies and masa harina in their satchels as a matter of course. On the road, instead of eating junk food, Kyle would find a Mexican dive and we'd eat black beans and rice, or she would cook, turning out things like chicken quesadillas on a tiny camping stove. Or else she'd say: fuck it, let's check into a crappy motel and drink cheap cocktails by the pool. But then, as soon as we arrived in San Francisco, she'd plan a dinner party – in some else's house, inviting folk we more or less happened upon.

I don't remember what it was she cooked for the dinner party, but what I do remember, and what I try to recreate fairly regularly, is what she'd do with tofu.

'Tofu?' I asked the first time she bought it. 'You are *choosing* to buy tofu?'

'Sure,' she said. 'Why not? And how about some ginger and a little sesame, and soy, of course, and these

avocados look ripe, and the broccoli is good.'

And then she'd spend about three minutes at some random stove producing something *completely* mouth-watering and refreshing that made me feel at peace with my body, which was a rare thing back then.

Kyle's surprisingly tasty tofu

Take a packet of **tofu** (the firm, rather than the silken kind) or however much you think you will eat, drain it of its water, then pat it dry with kitchen paper. You are frying the tofu, and any food that is to be fried must be perfectly dry. (You only have to think about the protesting spluttering that occurs when water meets very hot fat to remember this.)

Get the dressing ready, so that you can drizzle it on as soon as the tofu is ready. For two people (and this doesn't tend to be a dish you do for a large crowd) you need two tablespoons of **soy sauce**, two tablespoons of **rice vinegar**, one dessertspoon of **sesame oil**, a squeeze of **lime**, half a red **chilli**, deseeded and chopped very finely, and a nub of **ginger**, about the size of the top of your thumb, grated. (To grate ginger always use the finest grater you can find, such as a fine microplane. Special ceramic ginger graters are not that expensive to buy and you can get them quite easily.) Whisk together.

Cut the tofu into largish cubes – each cube should be about two bites worth, but no bigger. Sprinkle a small handful of plain flour onto a plate, season it with **salt** and **pepper**, and cover the tofu, on all sides, with the **flour**. Heat a tablespoon of **groundnut oil** or vegetable oil in a frying pan until it is very hot and cook the tofu (you may need to do this in batches if you are doing a lot) until it is a golden-brown colour on all sides. Remove from the frying pan and let it drain on kitchen paper.

Meanwhile, you could toast a few **sesame seeds** in a dry frying pan for a minute or two to use as a garnish.

When the tofu has drained place it onto plates with some greens. My favourite combination is a selection of **baby spinach, mustard greens, small cale** and **cavolo nero leaves**, half an **avocado** sliced as thinly as possible and a handful of **sugarsnap peas** that have been cooked very briefly in boiling salted water. A few florets of gently steamed **broccoli** are good, too. Place them next to the tofu and lightly dress both the tofu and the vegetables with the soy dressing and top with a few of the toasted sesame seeds.

I didn't tell Charles about my louche ways across the South and West of the US, at least not for a while. I went earnest instead.

'I wrote a piece about mothers and daughters for an Irish newspaper recently,' I lied. 'It's such a complicated and mysterious relationship after all.'

'Mothers and daughters?' Charles said, rolling his eyes. 'Are you serious? *How tired. Who cares?* What else?'

I had nothing else. I continued to lie, realising I needed to change track.

'Well,' I said. 'I wrote a travel piece about Miami Beach and its cult of fabulousness and how really it's all hideous because you can't get a chair lounger at the Delano Hotel unless you suck the pool guy's dick. But it was just a quick piece, really. A quick little satirical piece, not serious at all.'

'Oh,' said Charles. 'That sounds more like it. Or more fun, at least. Do you have the piece on you?'

'No,' I said. 'I don't carry my work with me.'

'Well maybe you should,' he said, annunciating each syllable carefully. 'Because here you are meeting an editor of *Vogue*, and it would have been quite handy to have it on you,

don't you think? But it's okay,' he said. 'You can fax it to me. Fax it to me tomorrow. And fax me your resumé, too. And Daisy?'

'Yes?'

'I'm the kind of person that if your resume has a typo, I burn it. I just burn it.'

That night I went back to the apartment and I wrote a piece about the Delano Hotel, and the next morning I faxed it to Charles. Only I spelt his last name wrong and I spelt Ian Schrager's name wrong *and* Philippe Starck's, but, in fact, Charles, for all his talk, is all heart and instead of burning anything he took me on. He gave me my first commission, helped me to get my first proper job, certainly got me my second job (when he left *Vogue* to be the features editor of Tina Brown's short-lived magazine *Talk* he took me with him), and taught me to write. He also leant me money, was generous with his prescription drugs, took me to parties and gay strip bars, listened to anything I had to say, constantly buoyed me up, always paid for dinner, and introduced me to other editors for whom I would soon write.

Hamish, Peter and my London family

One of those editors is called Hamish. We made friends in New York, but it was in London that we became close. I may have moved far away from Nell and my American friends, but Michael was in London, my sisters were both now in London, and Peter, Hamish's boyfriend, lived in London, which meant Hamish was frequently there, too. Through them I met their friends: Gordon, Thomas, Georgina, Vicki, Victoria and others. And I had old, dear friends that I reconnected with.

'I like London,' I kept telling myself. 'I don't miss New York at all. This is a new chapter of my life and why look back?'

Then I embarked on a love affair with a quintessential New Yorker, a filmmaker whose work entirely centered around telling New York stories. Naturally enough he was rarely in London, which suited me fine because it meant my romantic life, such as it was, was boxed away and separate and private and secret and I could be my squirrelly, weird, alone self – who knows why. Only I couldn't quite because I couldn't quite create my own little island in England the way I had in New York.

In England I was part of a family *all the time*, not just when I chose, and family life was thriving. Rose had had a son and would soon have another, and Bay's baby, Billy, would be born two years after Frankie, Rose's youngest. In-between, my own contemporaries were getting married and having their children. Pops, meanwhile, was frequently in and out of hospital because of a neurological disease, CNDP, which was paralysing bits of his body, that he bore, and still bears, with unbelievable good grace, and which we mostly ignore. (I don't know what it would take for us not to rely on Pops, but certainly no illness. One friend went to Somerset to stay and reported back: 'But it was extraordinary. Your father had some kind of fainting fit and nobody appeared to notice.') Nor was Pops the only one fighting disease.

Peter, Hamish's boyfriend, was diagnosed with prostate cancer. All around me everyone was gathering together, and, miraculously it seemed, I was gathered up, too. I spent most weekends either in Somerset with my family, or in Gloucestershire, where Peter and Thomas shared a house.

I discovered that I no longer had to present myself, or sing for my supper, or promote myself as festive and easy and shiny and bright; I didn't have to put on a show. Instead, I learnt, I had to do things like keep in touch, check in, not disappear. We all loved each other willy-nilly, and that was good, only what did one do then with so much time, not to mention neediness, and how, after stalking around the periphery for so long (or so I imagined), did one do intimacy? As in the real thing? Just for example?

Well, one way I did it was to stand at the stove or the kitchen counter and cook. Cooking is like a therapist's dream solution, or it was mine. Here is something that is completely absorbing, as challenging as you want it to be, open to fantasy and invention and creativity, and yet just as good kept simple. It requires only basic skill and knowledge, but every time you do it you learn more, which means that the more you do it the more you enjoy it, and the more you enjoy it the better the result.

You should behave, in the kitchen and towards your ingredients and your diners, with integrity and honesty. The more curious you are the better. Best of all, for me, was that I was doing something necessary. Instead of escaping, I was making food for the people around me.

After eight years of dining out that felt like a huge relief. It was also, I discovered, a way to relax into my own skin: to just be. My sisters are good at being affectionate and demonstrative and intimate, but I'm less adept. A chopping board and a recipe book seem to help.

Plus, sharing a kitchen counter with my mum every once in a while meant that we no longer had to have the twice-yearly catch-up chats over a Wagamama lunch that were always a bit awkward and more formal than either of us wished.

The ones where the conversation went along the lines of:

Her: 'So what have you been doing?'

Me: 'Working. Stuff.'

Her: 'Seeing friends?'

Me: 'Of course seeing friends.'

Her: 'Are you writing for yourself?'

Me, crossly: 'No. Not really.'

Her, once: 'Are you depressed?'

Me, furious: 'No.'

As in, yes. Depressed and fat and lonely and fine and unsure and lost and really okay and lazy and procrastinating and how do I turn the lights on? and when does it all start? all at once.

In the kitchen, the lights felt on. My mum would join me bustling round the kitchen and we'd listen to Radio 4 and wonder at someone's *Desert Island Disc* choices or see how quickly we knew who Michael Berkeley was talking to on *Private Passions*. Or shout at the dogs or make gravy together or whatever. No great shakes, but actually, sort of, really great shakes.

What would I cook? At the beginning, variations of things I'd learnt on the boat or seen Nell or Rose or Michael make in America: roast chicken, pasta with broccoli and courgettes, bruschetta, grilled fish, roasted vegetables, rack of lamb with a minty salsa verde and boiled potatoes slightly roughed up and sloshed with olive oil and a lot of parsley, green salads (but with proper dressing, instead of something murky and made in vast quantities that used to sit on the kitchen counter in Somerset in a kilner jar for weeks on end).

I started to buy cookery books (that habit has only got worse) and to try new things. I asked friends for recipes. When I had settled into my flat, my mum and Pops (in London for some reason or other) came to have a look around before driving back to Somerset together. It was late autumn and I made a light supper of Jerusalem artichoke and scallop soup from Simon Hopkinson's book, *Roast Chicken and Other Stories*.

This soup is one of the most successful and pleasing plates of food you can make, because it is perfectly balanced and satisfying, with a delightful extravagance (scallops! In soup! But this is a treat indeed!), but without being too pretentious or rich or having any kind of digestive kick-back. It also provided me with a signpost: 'Go *this* way,' the soup sang. Don't just get better and more confident at making the same things over and over again and then rely on them to feed you while you get on with the rest of your life. Instead, relish it. Learn more. Cook differently. Try things. Cook more.

Simon Hopkinson's Scallop and Artichoke Soup

from *Roast Chicken and Other Stories* by Simon Hopkinson

I don't always make croûtons, sometimes serving it with good bread instead, not that it needs any accompaniment at all.

Serves 4

50g butter

a large onion, peeled, finely chopped

300ml fish or light chicken stock

1 bay leaf

1 thyme sprig

450ml milk

225g Jerusalem artichokes,

peeled, coarsely chopped

salt and freshly ground black pepper

8 scallops, cleaned, roe intact, cut into large chunks

150ml double cream

2 tbsp chopped flat-leaf parsley

croûtons, to serve

1 Melt the butter and fry the onion until thoroughly soft without colouring. Add the stock, bay leaf and thyme, cover and simmer gently for ten minutes or so.

2 Add the milk and the artichokes, bring to the boil, season well and simmer until the artichokes are completely collapsed. You may find that the liquid has a messy separated look about it, but once it has been liquidised, it will all come back together.

3 Before processing the soup, strain off a large ladle of the liquid and in a small pan gently poach the scallops for a few seconds until just firm. Lift out with a slotted spoon, place on a warm plate and cover. Return the liquor to the soup, remove the thyme and bay leaf and liquidise.

4 Pass through a fine sieve, reheat with the cream and parsley and, finally, stir in the scallops to warm through. Serve with croûtons.

A further soup lesson:

Here, in a few lines, is the secret to making fantastic soup, taught to me by Rory O'Connell. In fact, here it is in three words: *sweat the vegetables*.

Sweating the vegetables is a way of cooking them, in butter or oil, so that they soften, sweeten up, and begin to release their flavours. What is crucial is that you then trap these flavours, so that nothing evaporates into either the pot or your kitchen. You do this by closely covering the vegetables (that have all been diced to the same size before you put them in the pan) with either a butter wrapper, if you have one handy, or a piece of greaseproof paper cut to the right size so that it fits snugly into your saucepan (this is called a cartouche). Then you put the lid on your saucepan and leave them to sweat. The heat must be very low or your vegetables will start to brown, which you don't want, as what you are after is a pureness of flavour.

Another tip for making any soup: if you are puréeing your soup, do it immediately the vegetables are cooked. Simply put, the sooner you purée everything, the more delicious the soup will be.

Potage bonne femme

Here is a classic leek and potato soup. This becomes Vichyssoise when served cold with added cream and chives. One thing about cold soup: make sure you serve it in smaller quantities than you would hot. Cold soup is delicious and everyone adores the first few spoonfuls; too much and it becomes a chore to eat.

This is a very handy recipe because once you have learned the basic techniques in it, you can use them to make any vegetable soup: Jerusalem artichoke, for example, carrot or parsnip.

First dice your vegetables, which for this soup are **onions**, **potatoes** (the base for most vegetable soups) and **leeks**. They should be the same size more or less, so that they take the same amount of time to cook, and they should be small: about ½cm square. A general guide in terms of amounts is to use about twice as much potato as onion, and three times as much leek. So, for this soup to serve four generously (or six perfectly adequately) you need 110g diced onions,

200g diced and peeled potatoes and 310g diced leeks.

Over a moderate heat, melt 60g **butter** in a largish saucepan that has a lid. Wait until it foams before adding all the diced vegetables, then season them with **salt** and freshly ground **black pepper**. Stir, so that they are coated in the melted, foaming butter. Add your greaseproof paper or butter wrapper lid directly on top of the vegetables, and then put the lid on the saucepan. Turn down the heat, and let the vegetables sweat for about ten minutes, until they are just beginning to soften and break down. You do not want to either brown or overcook the vegetables, so make sure the heat is gentle. And again: *make sure the heat is gentle*.

Add about 900ml of **chicken stock**, depending on how dense you like your soup (add a little more if you like it a bit looser). Put the lid back onto the saucepan (you are not trying to reduce the soup; that would make it too strong) and increase the heat, so that the stock with its veg. comes up to the boil, then turn it down so that it remains simmering. If you boil it too hard the vegetables will bruise. Simmer

until the vegetables are just cooked – taste them to check – and as soon as they are, purée everything immediately. I use a hand-held blender directly in the saucepan, which works well, and the rule is: puree the soup until you think it is completely smooth and then purée some more. Add some **full-fat milk** to achieve a consistency you like, and season the soup with **Maldon salt**, freshly ground **black pepper** and sprinkle with chopped **chives** or **parsley**.

For Vichyssoise

Let the soup cool completely, before adding about 300ml of cold cream and four large tablespoons of finely chopped chives. Chill it, then taste and correct the seasoning before serving it in *small* portions.

I met Thomas, and Gordon, in Morocco when Peter threw Hamish a week-long 40th-birthday party in Tangier. The first party of the week was at Gordon's house in the Kasbah, and the first thing Gordon said to me when I walked in, and this our very first meeting, was:

'So. How big? You might as well give it up. Because I know you know, girl.'

'*What*?' I asked. 'What are you talking about?'

'Oh please,' he said. 'Don't start with the naivety. Butter wouldn't melt. Puff Daddy's cock. How big?'

'Oh,' I said. 'Oh. Big. Did you doubt it?' That was my short cut to friendship with Gordon: sleeping with Puff Daddy, which means at least it was good for something.

But we became much closer very quickly for another reason and that reason was Peter and his battle against cancer.

Peter was the most loved person I have ever met, and blessed with every quality. He was sophisticated and debonair with matinee idol looks and he designed and built complicated interiors all over the world. He also

had a heart the size of a church, made all of us laugh all of the time, and discovered, when he began renting Spoonbed, the house in Gloucestershire, with Thomas, that what he really loved doing was home-making: cooking and gardening and jam-making and whatnot.

'What are you doing today?' he might ring up and say.

'Working,' I would reply. 'Deadlines. What about you?'

'I've taken the day off. I'm spending the afternoon with Constance Spry trying out canapés for the party next week. What are your thoughts about devils on horseback?'

'I'll be right over.'

And then we would spend the day experimenting with prunes and hot red wine and bacon (though how far can you go drowning prunes in alcohol, wrapping a rasher of bacon around each one and putting them into the oven? Not very. But the sampling was good). Or else we would sit round the kitchen table at Spoonbed, having picked buckets of damsons from the trees outside, discussing, when making jam, to stone or not to stone. Then we might play cards. They were happy days. Except that the reason Peter would take a day off work was because he had been to the hospital for a dose of chemo- or radiotherapy.

Peter did not consider defeat; never lost his sense of humour; was never less than sparkling company. In the New Year he and Hamish began to eat differently by following the cancer diet, which meant no dairy, no meat, no caffeine and no alcohol. Prunes, yes. Devilled and on horseback, no. Neither considered this new way of eating a particular deprivation (bacon Peter missed and the odd glass of wine), and when we were with them neither did we.

Hamish once rang me from an expensive fishmongers to ask what he should buy to take on the train to Spoonbed.

'Wild Sea Trout,' I sang out without hesitation. It was mid-March and just the beginning of it being in season. Later that evening, when we arrived in Gloucestershire, Hamish said: 'The trout, not all that much of it, cost £56. That seemed quite expensive to me, but you seemed so sure about getting it, so I did.'

He raised one eyebrow while he looked at me, not wholly amused. 'True or false, you knew it was the most expensive fish in the shop?'

He began to smile, the eyebrow getting higher.

'It will be worth it,' was all I could say, and it was. Though cerviche is usually made with firm white fish such as halibut or sea bass, we felt considering the price of the trout and the fact that we didn't have all that much of it, we had to eat it as purely as possible. We squeezed a couple of limes and lemons over it and let it sit in the fridge for a couple of hours 'cooking' in citrus fruit's juices, then ate it with a smidgen (you don't want to overpower the fish) of chopped red onion and coriander. No, it didn't feel like deprivation.

Berry compote jelly

I used to take jelly to Peter when he was in hospital, using different fruits as the weeks wore on. Blood orange was a favourite, but more popular still was the jelly I made using some of the syrupy juices, plus a bit of sieved fruit, from a berry compote (also the basis for berry ice cream). The red- and blackcurrants, blackberries and raspberries that we gather every summer in Somerset freeze well (and are quite cheap to buy frozen), so I make berry jellies, compotes and ice creams or sorbets all-year-round. No one ever seems to tire of them.

Making jelly

Once you understand a few rules, jelly is simple to make, especially if you use leaf gelatine. The first rule being knowing how much gelatine you need. It can be confusing because there are two different sizes of leaf gelatine available. One is quite a lot bigger than the other (though not quite double the size), and often recipes don't specify which size you should be using. The gelatine packets come with instructions on them, but if you are in a hurry, with various timings swimming around your head,

and you want to make enough jelly to fit a 700ml mould, then being told that fifteen leaves sets two pints of liquid is enough to send you over the edge.

The gelatine that you come across most frequently is the smaller sheets, and so this is the size that I refer to. Two of these smaller leaves are equal to one teaspoon of powdered gelatine, making it easy to substitute one for the other if your recipe calls for powdered gelatine. (You *can* use the powdered stuff, it's just that it takes a bit longer to prepare, as it needs to 'sponge' before being dissolved in a *bain marie*. But any recipe that calls for it should also provide you with clear instructions on how to do this.)

Leaf gelatine: the rules

One small leaf of gelatine will set 83ml of liquid, which is an impossible measurement and means you have to round things up somewhat. So, use four leaves to make 300ml or seven leaves to set a pint or just under 600ml of liquid. I have an old-fashioned jelly mould that needs 700ml liquid to fill it, and so I use eight and a half leaves of gelatine.

This makes enough to feed about six people (you serve jelly quite delicately; no one wants a huge walloping mass of it.) Alternatively, let it set in small ramekins or moulds or espresso cups.

Soaking

Once you have established how much gelatine you need, separate the leaves so that they are not stuck together, and soak them in a bowl of cold water for four or five minutes. Check that there are no hard bits by feeling the leaves with your fingers. They will have swollen up to a degree. Take them out of the water and gently squeeze as much excess water out as you can. They will still feel wet and slimy, and that's how they should be.

Dissolving the gelatine

Simply put, jelly is a combination of a sweetened liquid – a sugared syrup, elderflower cordial, apple juice, wine or champagne, juices from berries,

or anything else tasty (sloe gin, for example) – and gelatine, which has then been allowed to set. The sweetened liquid is usually (but not always) heated first, so that the sugar and then the gelatine dissolves completely into it. DO NOT boil the liquid. If you do heat the sweetened liquid, bring it close to boiling point before you add the gelatine, but don't allow it to boil, not at any point. The gelatine will know, and boiling liquid upsets its setting powers. If you don't heat the liquid, the gelatine still needs to be dissolved. In this case, put it, squeezed of its soaking water, into a saucepan over a low heat and stir occasionally. This takes less than minutes.

Combining

Always add the cold mixture (usually the soaked gelatine) into the hot one (usually your sweetened or flavoured liquid or syrup). Cold into hot. Always. This is so as to avoid lumpy jelly.

Adding fruit

If you are adding fruit – always appreciated – you will want it to be suspended in the jelly, rather than floating to the top (or the bottom when you turn it out) of the mould. Put some fruit – berries, say, or slices of orange – into an oiled mould (use a tasteless oil or line it with cling film), then pour in enough of your prepared liquid to nearly cover the fruit. Allow this to begin to set by putting it into the fridge for about forty-five minutes, and then pour in the rest of the jelly mixture, adding more fruit if you wish.

Berry compote jelly

I use a mixture of **redcurrants**, **blackcurrants** and **blackberries** and sometimes **raspberries**, depending on whether we still have any of the latter left in the freezer. Sometimes, early in the freezing season, there may be some loganberries, too. It doesn't really matter what berries you use; any of these, used in any proportion will be delicious. You'll need about a kilo of berries to make the jelly (which serves about six) which also means that you'll be left with plenty of fruit (you only use the juices) for a compote to eat either with it, or separately for breakfast, or to use to make a delicious berry ice cream.

Defrost the berries. Make a basic sugar syrup by mixing roughly equal amounts of granulated **sugar** and **water** together in a saucepan over a medium heat. Bring the mixture to the boil and let it simmer for a few minutes, stirring occasionally until all the sugar has dissolved. For a kilo of berries you will need about 225ml of water and 200g of sugar.

Place all the berries in a separate saucepan, add the sugar syrup and heat gently, giving it an occasional stir. I often squeeze half an **orange** or a couple of tangerines into the mixture, too, to slightly off-set the sweetness.

You don't want to boil the fruit, but let it cook gently for five to ten minutes. By this time the liquid will be a wonderful deep red colour. Taste it. Is it sweet enough? If it's not, then add a little more sugar; if you would rather it be more tart, squeeze in a little extra lemon juice.

Now squish about a quarter of the cooked berries through a sieve into a large measuring jug. This is quite hard work, but as you are not sieving all that many berries (compared to, say, ice cream for twelve) it won't take long. You then want to thin out this thick pulpy purée, so add just the juice from the saucepan to the measuring jug until you have 700ml (or however much you need for your mould) of liquid.

Now add eight and a half soaked and squeezed out (small-sized) **gelatine leaves**. The liquid should be hot enough to dissolve the leaves, so if it has cooled down, reheat it, without letting it boil, before adding the gelatine. Let the gelatine sit in the hot liquid for about ten minutes before giving it a stir to make sure it has all dissolved. Pour into a single or several smaller moulds and let it cool before putting it into the fridge to set, which will take about three hours.

I don't add any actual fruit to this jelly, as it is rich enough without it and the defrosted berries don't cry out for inclusion the way that fresh ones do – in which case I would make a lighter, clearer jelly base using, say, a sugar syrup flavoured with mint leaves and frambroise and suspend the berries in it.

When the jelly has set, boil some water and pour it into a large bowl. Dip the mould in the water for a just a few seconds to gently melt the outer edge of the jelly. It should slip out easily, but you may also need to create an air bubble between one side of the jelly and the mould for it to fall out. Wet one of your hands and just sort of ease your fingers into the jelly along its side to 'un-mould' it.

Vincenzo and Margarita

'Who made this cake?'

This is a friend called Patrick on a minibus to Stansted airport talking to his neighbour, Victoria. I am sitting behind them. Behind me is Thomas and Gordon. We are – fourteen of us – on our way to Puglia, in the heel of Italy, to celebrate Peter's birthday over a long weekend, a trip organised and paid for entirely by Hamish. It is April. Only Hamish and Peter aren't with us because Peter all of a sudden isn't well enough to travel. No one knows quite what to say and so mostly we talk about the picnic we have all contributed to, no part of which contains meat or dairy.

'I made it, yes. Of course I made it,' I hear Victoria say.

'It's terribly good,' Patrick says, 'how do you make it?'

I listen to Victoria's reply with interest, because in fact I made the cake, a carrot cake that contains no butter and has extravagantly huge lexia raisins in it instead of walnuts.

'Well, first you take the carrot, and then you...but I have something to tell you. You won't believe it...'

Patrick, however, was not to be put off so easily.

'Yes, but finish about the cake. Carrot, of course. What else?'

'Carrots. Lots of carrots. I use only organic. Harrods has very good ones. So. You grate the carrots. I'll write it down in Puglia. It's good, or non? Now, as I was saying, you won't believe it, Patrick...'

'No, no,' I heard Patrick interrupt briskly. 'No need to write it down. Just tell me. You grate the carrots, then what?'

And so the conversation continued until Victoria tossed her head, laughed and admitted that she hadn't made the cake. It is a scrumptious cake, though. Even Rose sees its point, and she, before this cake, was of the school that held: why make a carrot cake when there is chocolate available?

Best carrot cake for Peter

Makes about 12 slices

a little butter for greasing

300g self raising flour, plus a little for sprinkling

5 medium-large peeled carrots, which makes about 400g once grated

juice and zest of 1 small orange (a blood orange is best if they are in season)

160g good raisins such as lexia raisins, or else good sultanas.

$\frac{1}{4}$ tsp bicarbonate of soda

$\frac{1}{2}$ tsp baking soda

1 tsp ground cinnamon

$\frac{1}{2}$ tsp ground cloves

$\frac{1}{4}$ tsp grated nutmeg

$\frac{1}{2}$ tsp salt

4 large free-range eggs

250g golden caster sugar

300ml sunflower oil

for the icing

130g butter

$\frac{1}{2}$ tsp vanilla extract

250g cream cheese

100g icing sugar

1 Preheat the oven to 180°C/350°/gas mark 4. Line the bottom of two 23cm spring-form tins with baking parchment and lightly grease all over with a bit of butter, then dust the sides and bottom with a fine sprinkling of flour.

2 Grate the carrots into a bowl and add the orange zest. Put the orange juice into a separate bowl and add the raisins or sultanas so that they soak up some of the juice.

3 Mix together the flour, bicarbonate of soda, baking soda, cinnamon, ground cloves, nutmeg and salt.

4 Put the eggs and sugar into a large bowl and beat together, preferably using an electric mixer. Add the sunflower oil slowly while continuing to beat until everything is mixed together.

5 Add the carrots with their orange zest, give the mixture a stir, then sift in the flour and spices.

6 Fold everything together gently using a large metal spoon until just combined. You want to beat the mixture as little as possible at this point, so that the cake stays light.

7 Finally, fold in the raisins and any of the juice left in the bottom of the bowl.

8 Pour equal amounts of the mixture into the two tins and bake in the oven for about thirty minutes or until a skewer comes out clean.

9 Let the cakes cool in their tins for about ten minutes before turning them out onto a wire cake rack. Allow them to cool completely before icing.

To make the icing

Blend the butter, vanilla extract and cream cheese together well, then sift in the icing sugar and mix it in. It will have the consistency of a thick cream. Spread it on top of one cake, then sandwich the other on top and spread the rest over the top and sides of the cake. Chill the iced cake for two hours before attempting to cut it: this will firm up the icing nicely.

Peter died two months after the Puglia trip, at home in his bed, Hamish by his side. Not long afterwards Hamish and Thomas organised a tree-planting ceremony at Spoonbed, as well as a memorable funeral in London. The day before the ceremony was Hamish's birthday.

There were many of us staying at Spoonbed that weekend, sleeping on floors and sofas, sharing beds, and all of us cooked together. For Hamish's birthday supper – a dairy- and meat-free occasion, though the rules were relaxed when it came to champagne and tequila – we made gazpacho followed by poached salmon with mayonnaise, tiny new potatoes, broad beans from the garden, a green salad, and for pudding, baked white peaches with white peach sorbet and Claudia Roden's orange cake. Thomas and I had bought Peter an ice-cream (or sorbet, as we stressed) maker for his birthday. This was the first time it was being used.

The mayonnaise lesson

It took me all day to make the mayonnaise for Hamish's birthday supper – I did other things, too, of course, but basically the making of the mayonnaise never, ever, ended.

The reason was this: I knew you made mayonnaise by beating oil into egg yolks, very, very slowly, drop by drop. I knew that you stopped when it looked like mayonnaise. I had seen Nell do it in Shelter Island while at the table about to eat without a bother on her. I knew, even, that it was unwise to use only olive oil (mayonnaise made so richly scratches the back of your throat), but instead to combine it with something milder like groundnut oil. And I knew that, on this occasion, I needed to make enough mayonnaise for twelve people ('Don't skimp on the mayonnaise,' Gordon said to me before I began. 'Plenty of mayonnaise please'). It seemed obvious, then, that I would need five or six egg yolks.

This is what you need to know about making mayonnaise:

1 Use two egg yolks. Only ever use two egg yolks. That will make enough mayonnaise for almost any lunch, but if you think it won't, make two lots of mayonnaise using two lots of egg yolks. It will be hugely quicker than cracking four egg yolks into one bowl. Trust me. I know. If you only want a small amount of mayonnaise, still use two egg yolks. Having a bit more to work with is better than fiddling about with a single egg yolk. And mayonnaise keeps perfectly well in the fridge for several days if you have used fresh eggs.

2 Use good quality eggs at room temperature. If your eggs are of a superior quality, you pretty much can't curdle the mayonnaise.

3 Measure out the ingredients before you start. It's so much easier to pour oil from a measuring jug than from a bottle, and if you know that 250ml of oil is what you will need, and you have it poured into a jug, it takes away any guesswork

To make mayonnaise

Take two of the freshest, best **eggs** you can get and separate the yolks into a large bowl. Add one dessertspoon of smooth (rather than grainy) **Dijon mustard**, one of **white wine vinegar**, a generous pinch of **salt** and a few grinds of **pepper** – white if you've got it, but black is fine, too (I don't think it matters if you can see black pepper flecks in mayo). You can adjust these amounts depending on how mustardy you want your mayonnaise. Pour 250ml **oil** into a measuring jug. I think a combination of groundnut oil and olive works best and again, experiment with different ratios. I tend to use 200ml groundnut oil and 50ml olive oil, poured together into the measuring jug.

Whisk the egg yolks, mustard, vinegar and seasoning together and then begin to pour in the oil, drop by drop, whisking all the time. Try to whisk with your wrist rather than your whole arm, which requires a weird sort of concentration, but means everything aches less. After a bit, when things start to thicken up and emulsify you can add the oil a little bit faster, in more of a trickle, and finally in a very gentle stream. Don't get too cocky towards the end though, the mayo can still split. If this does happen there is a solution: put another egg yolk into a clean bowl, whisk it up with a good pinch of salt and start to whisk your split mayonnaise mix into it very slowly just as if it were oil.

When your measuring jug is empty and the mayonnaise is thick and wobbly, taste it. You can add more salt, pepper and lemon juice to taste, or water if you want it a little thinner. Mayonnaise is much more versatile and good-natured, once it is made, than people often realise. You can add chopped herbs or pesto to it or thin it out considerably using hot stock, so that it becomes more of a sauce – and then add chopped herbs or watercress.

A few crushed cloves of garlic (crushed with salt against the blade of a knife) added to the yolks at the start will give you a garlic mayonnaise.

A note: I make mayonnaise often – in summer sometimes every day. It never curdles, but then my mum keeps chickens in Somerset, so I have access to fantastic eggs. I make it in London, too, when I buy good free-range eggs and it behaves there as well. But last

summer, staying with friends, I offered to make the mayonnaise for my hostess's dinner party. It split. Reader, it split seven times. I knew, after the second split that I was not going to be able to make mayonnaise that day, and that should have been the end of it.

'No, no, keep trying,' my hostess said merrily, handing me a tray of eggs with deliberation. 'I've got masses of oil, too.' Nothing I did worked. It was just one of those things. Sometimes you have to give up.

Poaching a whole salmon
We poached a whole salmon for Hamish's birthday in a fish kettle, which is the right size for a whole, large salmon and means you can lift the bitch out without breaking it. I had often read and heard that you needed to make a court-bouillon to poach a salmon in – a sort of light stock made with water, wine, carrots, onion, celery and a bouquet garni. I now know better.

If you are lucky enough to get hold of an entire salmon (an extremely tasty fish) why would you mask its flavour? (Hamish's birthday salmon was a beauty that weighed 2 1/2 kilos, fed twelve of us amply, and cost a small fortune. Thomas paid.) All you need to poach a salmon (make sure you keep its head, tail and scales on) is salted water and a fish kettle, or, if the salmon is on the smaller side, an oval casserole or saucepan with a lid. The salmon should fit fairly snugly in the saucepan, rather than be swimming about in it.

What is important is the proportion of salt to water (basically, you are recreating sea water) and how much water you use. The rule is: use one tablespoon of salt for every 1.2 litres of water. How much water do you need? Put your salmon in the kettle or saucepan and add enough water so that it just covers the fish. That's how much. Take out the salmon, measure how much water you've got in a jug, add the correct amount of salt, then return the water to the saucepan or kettle.

Once you've sorted out the quantity of salted water that you need, bring it up to the boil in the pan or kettle. Gently put the salmon in, and then turn the heat down, so that the water just simmers. Put the saucepan or kettle lid on and continue to cook, at a simmer, for twenty minutes. Turn the heat off and let the salmon rest in the water for another five minutes. The salmon will be perfectly cooked. It doesn't matter how big the salmon is, as long as it is just covered by water, in a pan without loads of spare room, it will take twenty minutes to cook.

Carefully lift the salmon out – if you are using a kettle this is quite easy (though a lot easier with two people than one) and let it drain on the kettle's rack for a few minutes. If you are using a saucepan or casserole lift it out using two fish slices (or one of those nice wide ones that I've spotted online and got my eye on) and let it drain on a clean cake rack (or just hold it patiently; aching wrists are frankly a small price to pay compared to risking disaster by putting it down and picking it up again). Ease it onto a hot oval serving dish and put lots of parsley, watercress, fennel and lemon wedges around it. I take the skin off before taking it to the table, but you can just peel it back gradually as you serve it.

After Peter died and we had planted his tree and sprinkled his ashes at Spoonbed, I went first to Tangier with Gordon and Thomas, and then to southern Italy to stay with Jackie and Jay, who had rented a villa on the coast near Maratea. Friends of theirs, a Sicilian couple called Vincenzo and Margarita, arrived one morning on their motorcycle, Gina from Messina, and immediately offered to cook.

'It will be amazing,' Vincenzo said about the meal we would eat later that day. 'You won't believe it,' he added matter of factly. None of us doubted him.

Much of the day was spent procuring goodies; the kitchen in the rented villa was examined closely to see how far it could be stretched, and our afternoon on the beach was cut short so that Jay and I could be drafted in to scrub a couple of sinks-worth of mussels. All day, led by Vincenzo, we talked of nothing else but the forthcoming evening meal. You could feel the excitement even in the grains of Maratea's black sand: Vincenzo is cooking. Vincenzo is cooking tonight. Electricity crackled. The sky darkened. And so on.

Margarita, meanwhile, smiled benevolently at her love's fabulous promises. Vincenzo was the cook, she said, but she was happy to run up a Tiramisú for dessert.

Pause here. Pause to remember Margarita's tiramisú.

Vincenzo made pasta with mussels and it was delicious. The climax of the cooking was when he cooked the pasta as if it were risotto rice, in just enough mussel stock for each piece of spaghetti to absorb and cook to perfection. Not a noodle needed to be drained. This required much stirring of much pasta, precision timing and, as Vincenzo kept reminding us, nerves of steel. The pasta was all the better for it. There was no question about that.

'But not *that* much better,' Jay said quietly the next morning. 'It was still spaghetti with mussels, like we had in the little café by the beach. For all the talk...' he trailed off, caught in deep thought. I knew what he was thinking.

'Margarita's tiramisú?' he said, his voice brightening. 'Which, by the way, may be the most delicious thing I've ever eaten, is there any more of that by any chance? Or did we eat it all already?' We had eaten it all already.

When I asked Margarita about her tiramisú she admitted that it was a special recipe that had been passed down through generations of women in her hometown, and taught to her very precisely. She then taught it to me, which involved making it again, which meant that we ate it for breakfast and tiramisú, it turns out, works as a breakfast dish. Who knew?

There are two tricks to Margarita's version. One is using the right kind of biscuits and those aren't ladies fingers or savoiardi biscuits, but a much thinner, more delicate biscuit called a Pavesani. You can get these inexpensive biscuits, not at specialist delis or posh food halls, but at any Italian grocer, or online. The second trick is in the timing. Each biscuit must be soaked in its coffee and liqueur soup for four seconds on each side.

'What do I do if I can't find Pavesani biscuits in England,' I asked Margarita, before I knew how easy it was to find them, once you knew where to look. 'Can I use savoiardi biscuits instead? You see them everywhere.'

'Well,' she said. 'You could. But the timing is completely different for those biscuits. And you will make a quite different tiramisú.' She wouldn't be drawn further on the matter.

On the subject of creamy desserts from other countries, a word: Bløtkake. Bløtkake (pronounced blert-cark-er) is a sponge, cream and strawberry layer cake covered in marzipan and usually heavily decorated, that is eaten on special occasions in Norway. You invite someone to dinner there and they might bring a Bløtkake. At least that's what happened when I was in Norway, staying with my friend Becky who is a quarter Norwegian and has lots of family there. The Bløtkake she was given looked too fabulously garish to be delicious. How wrong one can be. Bløtkake is the lightest and frothiest cake it the world. It is a slightly vulgar but extremely seductive Paris hat of a cake.

When I make Bløtkake now, for a summer tea party, or for after lunch, I always think back to a pudding I made, shortly after getting off the boat, which didn't work at all. It was a white chocolate and raspberry tart – very 2002 – and it was horrible. It tasted rich and soapy and only took about twelve hours to make. I remember thinking, even at the time, but why have I made such a thing? Why have I buried the raspberries in white chocolate, which nobody really likes and, moreover, *white* chocolate mixed with butter and cream? Why haven't I just produced fresh raspberries and a jug of cream. Or a fruit tart, but without chocolate. Or chocolate, fine, but a pudding using proper, real, dark chocolate. Why did I choose the tart? Because I thought it would be one of those things that would be unexpected: a journey of taste explosions promoting untold delights, a white tart, but, oh, it's chocolatey, and oh, there are raspberries, and oh, Daisy can make pastry! I wanted to show my guests I could be relied on to make a *pudding*.

Bløtkake is actually what I should have made, if I had known about it then. It delivers more than it appears to offer, not that its kitsch appearance is to be scoffed at. It's just so surprisingly light and that surprise is a very effective ingredient.

So, too, of course, are those classics: sponge cake, raspberries, strawberries, freshly whipped cream and marzipan. The lesson was: what do you want to eat? Cook what you want to *eat*.

Margarita's tiramisú

You will need a square dish to make the tiramisú in. I use the same one I use for lasagne, which always makes Mum laugh. It measures 35cm x 22cm. The tiramisú will take about four hours to set in the fridge, but it is best made the night before.

serves 8–10

5 good free-range eggs
180g sugar
500g mascarpone
a pot of strong coffee
3-4 tbsp of brandy or, if you
    can get it, an Italian coffee
    liquor called Caffe Borghetti
a pinch of salt

about 300g of Pavesini
    biscuits (the exact amount
    depends on the size of your
    dish. You will need to buy,
    though not use entirely,
    two packets)
grated chocolate or chocolate
    flakes, or, at a push, good
    cocoa powder

1 Separate the eggs. Beat the sugar with the egg yolks, preferably with an electric whisk or in a mixer until the mixture turns pale.

2 Add the mascarpone, one 250g packet at a time, to the egg-and-sugar mix, and beat again. Add two tablespoons of coffee and one or two tablespoons of alcohol and continue blending until the mixture is smooth. It will turn a beautiful pale chestnut colour. Taste it. You can always add more coffee or alcohol, but it shouldn't taste overpoweringly of either.

3 Add a pinch of salt to the egg white and beat them until stiff peaks form.

4 Add the whisked egg whites to the mascarpone, egg and sugar mix and beat for a few minutes until the mixture becomes runny like a thick cream (don't worry about deflating the air out of the egg whites: you don't need it).

5 Pour the coffee into a flat container and add one or two tablespoons of alcohol. Caffe Borghetti, which you can only get at very good liquor shops, packs less of a punch than brandy, so you can use a little more of it – sometimes as much as three or four tablespoons if your coffee is very strong. Just keep tasting.

6 Line your dish with a layer of the cream mix – not more than a third of it. Soak each Pavesani biscuit in the coffee mixture for four seconds on each of its two sides, and lay them out in neat horizontal rows on top of the cream. Try to leave as few gaps as possible. You may need to cut a few of the biscuits in half to get into the corners of the dish.

7 Cover the layer of biscuits with a second layer of the cream, then cover this layer of cream with another layer of soaked biscuits, only this time lay them out in vertical rows. Cover with a final layer of the cream.

8 Let it sit in fridge for minimum four hours. Overnight is best.

9 Immediately before serving cover the tiramisú in a thin layer of grated dark chocolate. If you are using cocoa instead of grated chocolate, use it sparingly. Too much creates a powdery finish, which will make you cough when you eat it.

Bløtkake or Norwegian cream layer cake

Serves 6–8

for the sponge base
5 good free-range eggs
125g sugar
125g plain flour
1 tsp baking powder

for the filling
6-9 tbsp of sherry, orange juice
    or milk
700g whipped cream, just stiff

500g crushed (use a fork)
    raspberries or strawberries
    or a combination of the two

for the decoration
250g marzipan
a tube or two (or three or
    four) of different coloured
    'writing icing'

1 Grease a 24cm spring-form cake tin and preheat the oven to 175°C/347°F/gas mark 4.

2 Whip the eggs and sugar until light and fluffy. Sift the flour and baking powder into this mixture and fold everything together carefully. Pour into the greased tin.

3 Bake on the lowest shelf of the oven for about thirty minutes or until a skewer inserted into the centre of the cake comes out clean.

4 Let the cake cool a little before removing it from the pan, then cool completely on a wire rack.

5 Divide the cake horizontally into three layers.

6 Take the top layer of the cake and use it as the base, baked side down, so that the side facing up is perfectly flat. Sprinkle a few tablespoons (two or three) of sherry, orange juice or milk (choose whichever one suits your tastes) over the sponge and then cover with a third of the whipped cream and a third of the crushed fruit.

7 Repeat with the middle slice (sponge, then sherry/juice/milk, cream and fruit) then top the cake with the bottom layer of sponge, baked side up.

8 Before spreading the last third of cream and fruit over the top and sides of the cake (the sides need cream only), measure the size of the cake with a piece of string. Trail the string up one side of the cake, across its top, and down the other side. This is so you know how much marzipan to roll out.

9 Roll out the marzipan in a large circle that will fit over the entire cake. It should be a little bigger than the length of the string to take account of the final layer of cream and fruit. Cover the entire cake in this last layer of cream and fruit – it will be a little thinner than the layers inside the cake and that is fine.

10 Carefully pick up the marzipan by draping it over the rolling pin and place it gently over the cake and smooth out any ruffles that may occur where it falls down the sides with the back of a spoon. The marzipan will cover the cake more smoothly than you might anticipate. You should just be able to tuck the edge of the marzipan under the cake where it meets the board or plate.

11 Decorate using tubes of icing. Some writing, a few squiggles and curlicues will do to make it look suitably garish.

A harder lesson

Eating alone. Cooking for one. How boring is this? When I am in Somerset or Gloucestershire or anywhere in company, I like to spend as long as possible cooking and eating. All weekend preferably, with a walk fitted in somewhere, and, if in Gloucestershire, a game of cards or two. But cooking alone? For myself? When I started cooking in London I had little truck with it. I wanted the whole thing done instantaneously in one quick motion from fridge to stomach, and, at the same time, once I had started eating I didn't want the meal, such as it was, to ever end. But eating a hunk of cheese and a bit of bread while standing up and leaning over a kitchen counter and reading the newspaper doesn't quite work. An hour later you feel unsatisfied and empty, and bloated and heart-burny.

Bread and cheese is fine, of course, and often delicious. But *sit down* I had to tell myself. Lay a place at the table. Drink some water. Calm down. Cut up a few tomatoes and let them sit for a moment or two in some salt and olive oil and torn up basil if you've got it. Get out the chutney if the cheese calls out for it. Hell, make a green salad. Do a bit more: poach an egg, and while you are at it, fry up a bit of bacon and deglaze the pan with a drop or two of vinegar and pour that over your greens and sit the egg on top.

Or steam or lightly boil a few florets of broccoli – purple sprouting broccoli, preferably – or some cavolo nero or chard or spinach (dry the greens really well once you have cooked and drained them. I wrap them up in a clean tea towel and blot them with it). Toast some pumpkin or sunflower seeds or a handful of pine nuts in a dry pan, and add them to the greens, too, with some olive oil and salt and pepper and a squeeze of lemon to the greens, along with a few shavings of Parmesan or some prosciutto. Rub a slice of garlic over a piece of toast along with a smattering of salt and a little olive oil. Do any of these things and you've got a meal.

I still have to force myself to spend ten minutes – ten minutes! – making myself lunch or dinner, but I do now do it. Puy lentils are a standby, and feta cheese and Parmesan are always in the fridge; bacon or pancetta, wrapped up two slices at a time, I keep in the freezer. Rice! I say to myself. Remember rice. Rice takes minutes to cook. So does couscous. So does quinoa. So does pasta. There is no rule that says you can only cook these things if you are not alone. Rice with peas from the freezer and a bit of parsley or mint or spring onions sliced up quickly or sautéed shallots makes a delicious lunch. So, of course, does an omelette, only I find you have to tell yourself that eggs are rich and that you are in fact full before your body catches up and you feel pleased with life.

If I'm working from home all week then I'll make soup on a Monday and eat it throughout the week. I have learnt that if you are alone, you *can* turn the oven on. It is allowed. You turn it on and then you go back to work or get on with your chores and

fifteen minutes later you chop up and peel half a butternut squash, say, (or an aubergine or some carrots or courgettes) and you put it into a roasting tray and sprinkle it with fresh thyme, Maldon salt, black pepper and olive oil, mix it all together with your hands (this takes about two minutes) and put it back into the oven until its done, which takes about forty minutes, while you continue with your day. When you take it out of the oven you put some lettuce or spinach leaves into a bowl with the squash and you add whatever you fancy: seeds or feta or Parmesan or bacon or ham or herbs or a combination of these things. You dress it with a little vinegar and oil and check that it is seasoned correctly, just as you would if you were making it for a lover or a friend.

You eat it slowly. You enjoy it. You then get up from the table without feeling mournful. If you live alone, food is company, which is, perhaps, one reason why it's easier to gobble it up half formed; it feels as though taking time to eat a meal might be a mark of loneliness, which it shouldn't be. It's also why you never want it to end.

Also, no one is watching you. That can be a pleasure, but it can also mean that, since your manners and behaviour go unmonitored, you might behave sloppily or eat too much. That, when indulged in and celebrated can be fabulous and relaxing, but when it happens as habit it becomes wearying and depressing and those feelings are isolating.

I think what I am trying to say is that after ten years of being single I realised I was profoundly lonely. Sure, I dated people and had adventures, but what is also true is this: my longest romantic relationship in ten years lasted four months. I had much in my life, but regular daily intimacy? Waking up or going to sleep next to someone I loved, eating a simple supper with someone without having to make arrangements or telephone calls? Someone else using the pepper grinder or making the toast or answering the telephone or running me a bath? I knew nothing of these things. I cooked either for eight or twelve or fourteen people, or else for one.

Chapter six
The happy ending.
Meals with my family,
setting up home, and
suppers for two

Cooking for two

And then I met someone. I met someone called Nick who not only liked coming to Somerset, but seemed happy to sit in the vegetable patch with me and, while I picked beetroot, sort out with painstaking care the good leaves from the coarse ones, so that they could later be part of a salad.

I met him by wandering into the right party. I was about to wander out again when my hostess said, 'Don't leave quite yet because there's someone I want you to meet,' and I became dizzy with weird expectation. I remember thinking: typical, here I am about to meet the love of my life and I'm wearing a horrible old mackintosh.

It didn't seem to matter. And, oh my God, life is easier when you're with someone. No one tells you this, or at least no one said it to me, but I was single for ten years and so I know: living alone, once the novelty wears off, is a fucking nightmare. There's no other way to put it. It's exhausting. You have to make plans all the time just to do basic things like seeing other human beings. You have to chivvy yourself to bathe regularly,

change your sheets, not grow horns, and not go mad with longing. You have to remind yourself to cook properly because the alternative (a whole packet of cream crackers and a hunk of cheese, or whatever) is sort of undignified and sort of awful, even if it is *so much* easier.

Cooking for two is eight-hundred-thousand times more inspiring. I wish this wasn't true, and for some perhaps it isn't. And now when I'm alone, although I don't run up anything even vaguely elaborate, I do make salads and roast vegetables and shave Parmesan and cook eggs and boil pasta and make soup. But back then all those things seemed weirdly impossible. No wonder I didn't learn to cook until I got on that boat. Bother for myself? Pin on a pinny and sing a song as I stir a sauce? My God, it took all my energy to get up and out the door.

But now, with Nick, I come home from working at the library or from some assignment and the evening is taken care of. We talk and watch the news and have dinner. It's easy. At the beginning I felt as if I'd emerged from ten years of treading the boards in musical theatre – *eight shows a week darling! How do we do it!?* – only minus the applause, payslip, and on top of a day job. No wonder I sought solace in a few strange beds back then. Frankly, I feel I behaved like a Saint relative to the circumstances. Nick and I aren't together every night, not by a long shot. We lead our own lives, as well as the one we are making together – but these days the week has its own rhythm without me having to get out the frigging tap shoes.

So too does the cooking. Cooking for two is ideal. The prep time is short because you don't have to chop much, which means you get to the cooking part faster. And unlike a lunch in Somerset for twelve or fourteen, timing matters less. There's no pressure. You might plan to eat at 8:30 but 9 is fine, too. And so is 9:30. And so is not tonight darling I can't be hashed.

Only it's quite easy to be hashed when all you have to do is buy a couple of fillets of fish and slap them, skin-side down, on a really hot griddle pan, for a few minutes, then turn them over, meanwhile washing some lettuce leaves and making a dressing or simmering a couple of handfuls of

puy lentils in water and dicing up a tomato or two and some herbs to mix into them. Or just slicing a lemon in half and putting the salt and pepper on the table. Fillets of fish are much easier when you are cooking for small numbers, and so are lamb and pork chops and so is steak. A) all these things are far more affordable and, B) you have enough room on your grill or in your oven. For instance:

Lemony pork chops, from *River Café Cook Book Easy*

Heat a grill pan until it is really hot and heat your oven to 200°C/400°F/gas mark 6. Put two **pork chops** onto the grill pan. Sprinkle the exposed sides with **salt** and **pepper**, while the sides on the heat seals. Turn them over. Salt and pepper the newly exposed sides.

Cut a **lemon** in half, then put the chops in a roasting tray, squeeze over the lemon and throw the squeezed halves into the tray with the chops. Roast for ten minutes. Baste the meat by squashing the lemon halves over the chops and spooning over any juices in the pan. Roast for a further ten minutes and eat with boiled potatoes or a slice of good bread and some greens.

This is so *easy*. But in Somerset, for eight or twelve or fourteen? It's just not possible, unless it's summer and the barbeque is out, but even then I don't want to buy that many chops – it's just not economical. But then you do others things down there: you don't, for example, roast a whole shoulder of pork for 24 hours unless you are cooking for many.

You do, though, roast a whole chicken. That's another thing about cooking for two: everything goes a long way. Like any sensible person, I spin a roast chicken into at least three good meals. There is the luscious roast one night – usually, if it's for two of us, with rice rather than potatoes (just as chops suit small gatherings, roast potatoes require more of a crowd), and a green salad. Then there is at least one or two meals made from the stock – a soup, a clear broth or a risotto. And then there is a third meal using up the leftover chicken, either by making it into a salad with mayonnaise, or warming it through in a teriyaki sauce and serving it with spinach leaves and rice. This produces a very welcome little meal.

Chicken teriyaki with rice and spinach

Peel and finely slice a piece of **ginger** about the size of the top of your thumb, so that you're left with thin matchsticks. Slice a small white or yellow **onion** in half through the root, then shred each half into fine half-moon slices. Cut up or pull from the carcass as much of the leftover cooked **chicken** as the two of you will eat (or that you have) into generous bite-sized pieces. Put about four handfuls of **basmati rice** into a large saucepan of salted water and bring to the boil. Let it cook until it is ready – which will take about twelve minutes – but taste a few grains to check. Drain it through a sieve and run warm water through it, which will stop it clumping together. It can then sit happily in the warm saucepan, rinsed of any starch, until you are ready to eat.

While the rice is cooking put 75ml **white wine**, 50ml of **soy**, 50ml of **mirin**, the sliced ginger, three dessertspoons of **caster sugar** and 50ml of **water** into another smaller saucepan over a medium heat and stir so that the sugar dissolves. Bring to the boil and simmer for a couple of minutes.

Add the onion half-moons and simmer for another five minutes until the onion is soft. Add the chicken and warm it through for two or three minutes – ensure it's properly hot, though.

Put the rice into two large bowls and top with **baby spinach** leaves. Spoon on the chicken and ladle on plenty of the hot broth, which will wilt the spinach leaves and soak through, flavouring the rice.

Chicken broth
Chicken broth is really just a very good chicken stock with sliced vegetables added to it, and any pieces of leftover chicken.

I usually sauté the vegetables first (1cm-thick slices of **potato**, **carrot**, **celery**, **onion** and **leek**) in **olive oil**, rather than just throwing them into the broth, as this caramelises them and makes the soup extra tasty. (This tip was taught to me by a gifted Italian called Saskia, a staggeringly good Tuscan cook.) Sauté the vegetables in batches (if you crowd the pan they will steam and cook in their juices), seasoned with **salt** and **pepper**, then drain them on kitchen paper. You may

need to change the oil once or twice. You will use a good deal of oil and kitchen roll, but it's worth it.

Once the vegetables are sautéed, cover them with the **chicken stock**, and add a sprig of **thyme** and two whole **cloves**. Simmer gently until the vegetables are soft, which will take fifteen to twenty minutes. Add any leftover chicken pieces towards the end of the cooking time so that it warms all the way through.

For a heartier soup, you can add farro or spelt or pearl barley – cook it first (and farro needs soaking, too) in simmering water until it is tender to the bite, before adding to the broth.

And for something more aromatic, add a couple of blades of lemon grass (smash the thicker end with something effective, like the blunt edge of a cleaver or a mallet) to the stock, as well as some slices of red chilli, some torn mint leaves and coriander and some sliced greens, like bok choi or spinach.

Cook some noodles briefly in boiling water (they need literally a minute or two) and put them into your soup bowls before spooning the scented broth over them. A squeeze of lime is also a very good thing.

Chicken stock

Of course, a good chicken broth is dependent on a good chicken stock, and a good chicken stock is easily made, it just needs a little care. You should absolutely want to drink the stock just as is, even while it is cooking.

Gather your **chicken bones**. If you had a roast chicken you'll have the carcass and bones from that, but keep all chicken bones and freeze them until you're making stock. If I am ever buying boned thighs from the butcher I will ask for the bones and keep them in the freezer. It doesn't matter whether the bones have been cooked or are raw, they can go into the pot together.

Add an **onion**, peeled, and cut into quarters, a large **carrot**, peeled and cut into three or four large chunks, a good lot of **celery** (certainly a couple of stalks and sometimes I add a whole head, including the leaves), again, cut into large chunks, a handful of **parsley stalks**, ten whole black **peppercorns** and a sprig of fresh **thyme**. If I've got **leeks** I'll add a couple, washed first, cut into two or three pieces. Cover everything with cold water (it is very

important to use cold water as it is while the water comes to the boil that it draws the flavours out of the bones and vegetables). Don't use more water than you need to just cover everything. Bring to the boil. Keep a slotted spoon nearby to skim off any nasty looking white bubbly bits – the scum – that rises to the top of the pot. Once it has reached a boil, turn the heat down to a simmer and put a lid on the pot, tilted at a slight angle, so that air can escape.

It is important to get your stock's temperature right. If you boil the stock hard your ingredients will disintegrate and your stock will be muddy, but if the water is too cool everything will just sit there wanly. The water in the stock should be gently bubbling. Simmer for anything from an one-and-a-half to three hours. Let everything cool in the pot and then strain through a sieve.

Stock freezes very well. Plastic milk containers are very good for this, once they have been well washed and sterilised with boiling water, because you can cut them open straight from the freezer and defrost the stock by heating it gently in a small saucepan. This means you can use stock from frozen, without having planned ahead.

Cooking for two can get a bit dinkety-doo, though can't it? It's relaxing and easy and lovely, but truth be told it's more pottering than cooking. Not like cooking in Somerset. Boom! That's cooking! There, when we're all together, it's eight or ten or twelve or fourteen every day for lunch for days in a row. That's when I live between the garden and the kitchen and wonder what I think I'm doing when I'm anywhere else.

Our constant summer lunch

This is the best meal I will ever cook, though in fact the actual cooking is the least of it. Mostly it involves picking, scrubbing and washing vegetables, and podding broad beans. Still, even though it looks like a few salads and an omelette, it takes a long time and many hands to get it to the table. And that's part of its charm.

To pod the broad beans, you need people. Last summer, a family friend called Will, Pops and Bay were given one sack of beans. They sat on a garden bench. Nick and Rose and Georgie, Rose and Tom's eldest son, on the front lawn were given another.

The two Toms, a third. Mum was exempted because she does, day in and day out, eight million other chores in the house – as in running it. A radio was switched on. Everyone gossiped. Everyone talked. The beans ruled. I boiled water and just as everyone thought their work complete I gave them back their beans, now blanched, for re-podding out of their inner skins. Yes, Rose, the small ones, too.

On washing carrots and beetroot and potatoes and lettuce: I do this alone immediately after picking them. It takes a long time. It involves much scrubbing. The lettuces require careful and thorough drying. This is the sort of dog work that for the most part goes unacknowledged by those who don't do it. What does everyone think I am doing up in the garden shed alone all that time? Needless to say I am never happier.

Courgette blossoms in beer batter

I never stuff these. Why would you? Their lightness is their point. They are best eaten on the fly, hot out of the pan, just as everyone is gathering for lunch or in the late

afternoon with a cold beer. In hot weather the flowers seem to bloom out of the courgette patch hour by hour. Every time Pops eats these, which is sometimes twice daily, he asks the same thing. 'Tell me, can you order these in a restaurant?' I tell him no, I am the only person in the world who can make them.

To make the batter, mix a small can of **beer** (any lager will do) with 150g of plain **flour**, a teaspoon of **salt** and 150g of **ice cubes** (which is about seven). The ice cubes make the batter lighter, because the coldness of the mixture means that it bubbles up nicely when it hits the hot oil. Mix everything together with a spoon – very small lumps are not only fine, they are preferable – and leave it to sit for a few minutes. Dip the blossoms into the batter, swirl them about a bit, let any excess batter drip off, then fry them in about half a centimetre of really hot **olive oil** in a sauté pan. They will take only about one or two minutes each side to cook. Drain them on kitchen paper and sprinkle with **Maldon salt** and fresh black **pepper**. Serve immediately.

Broad beans, peas and prosciutto

This is probably my summer desert island dish. It depends on fresh broad beans and peas, and there is no point giving amounts for this recipe, because it depends how many you are feeding or how many beans or peas you've got. I fill my wide sauté pan full with as many podded beans as I can. The peas are a bonus, but not essential. If I have pancetta I'll use it as well as the prosciutto. If I have any artichokes then I'll blanch them for five minutes, peel them down to their hearts, and use them too. It's an embarrassment of riches, this dish.

Begin by heating a generous mixture of **olive oil** and **butter** in the bottom of a heavy, large sauté pan. When your fat is hot, begin to gently fry some onion. I try to use tiny whole **white button onions** if I have them, but, otherwise, I'll finely chop two red onions and use them instead. If you have some **pancetta**, throw in some cubes or slices of it at this point and let it cook briefly, so that the fat melts down a bit and it begins to colour (I use less butter at the beginning in this case). Add the **artichokes**, if you're using them, at this stage, too, and a small handful of fresh **mint leaves**. Gently push the onion and artichoke hearts around until they begin to turn light brown. Add the **peas** and enough water to just about cover them. Place a thick slice of prosciutto on top of everything (if it's already sliced thinly when you buy it, it doesn't matter, but then you might go wild and use two slices). Simmer for about twenty minutes, or until the peas are cooked. Keep an eye on it, and stir it around every now and then. (Make sure that the water doesn't disappear on you. You can always add a bit more water if the pan is getting too dry too quickly. I like it to be quite dry, though, by the time the peas are cooked.)

Remove the slice of prosciutto, which will have done its work imparting its flavour to your cooking water. This is when I throw in a tablespoon or two of **sherry vinegar**, then a ladleful more of water or, even better, **chicken stock**. Now add your **broad beans** (already blanched and pinched out of their inner skins). The beans need heating through rather than actual cooking. To finish, season with **Maldon salt** and **black pepper**, some more mint, chopped, if you think it could do with it, more prosciutto (thin slices torn up or cut into ribbons) and a generous sloshing of olive oil.

Tortilla

I never leave enough time to cook this, which is a mistake. It's easy enough, but do not try to rush it. This is not the type of omelette that can be rustled up at the last minute, because it is only by cooking the potatoes slowly in the oil that you achieve the crucial creaminess. The quality of a tortilla is also dependent on really good eggs.

Heat about six tablespoons of **olive oil** in a large non-stick frying pan over moderate heat. Peel 450g of **waxy potatoes** and slice them very thinly. I do this on a mandolin, but by hand is fine, it will just take longer. Do not put the potatoes in water as you slice; you want to hold on to the starch. Add the potatoes and a thinly sliced **onion** (a white one is best, but it doesn't really matter) to the pan and stir until everything is completely coated in oil.

Reduce the heat so that it's quite low and cook, stirring often so that the vegetables do not colour, until the potatoes are cooked through – which is about fifteen endless minutes of stirring. The potato slices should remain separate, rather than glued together in a mushy mass. Remove the potatoes and onion with a slotted spoon and put them on something large like a baking sheet, lined with kitchen roll.

Pour the oil out of the pan into a cup (you won't have that much), wipe out the pan and remove any bits of potato or onion debris stuck to it. Take three tablespoons of oil from the cup – if you have enough in there, if not then supplement it with fresh oil, and put it back in the pan. Meanwhile, beat six free-range **eggs** lightly, as if you were making a normal omelette. Carefully transfer the potato and onion to a shallow bowl and pour the beaten eggs over them, turning the mixture over so that everything gets well coated. Season with **salt** and freshly ground **black pepper** and let everything stand for ten minutes.

Heat the oil in your pan until it is very hot, but not smoking, then add the potato and egg mixture, spreading it out evenly. Reduce the heat, and shake the pan often to prevent sticking.

After about ten minutes – when the top is no longer liquidy – cover the pan with a large, flat plate and turn the tortilla out onto the plate, using both hands and oven gloves. Do this quite smartly. It *will* work and is very satisfying. Add two more tablespoons of oil to the pan and return the tortilla, cooked-side up, to the pan. Do this by sliding it off the plate – hence the importance of it being flat. I have done it on a plate with a lip, but it's not very tidy and you sacrifice some of the as-yet-uncooked egg mix. Cook for about five minutes more, or until the underside is just browned and whole thing is cooked through. You can eat it hot or leave to cool to room temperature. Your brow will need mopping.

When ready to serve, sprinkle with **flat-leaf parsley** or **chervil** or torn **basil** or a mixture of all three, a little **Maldon salt** and some good **olive oil**. Take to the table on the flat plate you used for the turning business and slice it like a cake.

Tortilla is also great sliced but not separated, wrapped in wax paper and aluminium foil, and taken on a picnic.

Berry ice cream

When Nick first ate this in Somerset, where I make it frequently, he offered to buy me my own ice cream maker to use in London. I told him I didn't want my own ice cream maker and muttered something about berry ice cream being a Somerset treat because it is there that we harvest berries all summer long (or so it seems) and consequently, as well as eating as many as possible fresh, have a freezer-load of red- and blackcurrants, blackberries and raspberries for the rest of the year. This is reason enough to churn it into ice cream, never mind how *incredibly delectable* the ice cream is.

The high density of fruit is why it works so well. The disadvantage is that to make it without grimacing at the price of buying so much fruit, you need to have access to a few currant and/or berry bushes. Using blackberries alone is delicious if that's what you can gather most easily. I tend to use more blackcurrants in my mix than anything else because we have so many of them.

But the fruit issue wasn't actually why I refused the ice cream maker. The reason was because I didn't have room for it in my kitchen. I didn't have room for an eggcup in my kitchen. This might have been because a lot of space was taken up by my bowl collection.

I never meant to collect bowls. I just bought them, mostly from junk shops and flea markets, one by one. I didn't notice what was happening – a bit like putting on weight – until one day I had to wrap each one up to put them all into storage. Nick and I had decided to look for a house to buy together, which meant I was temporarily moving into his flat. There wouldn't be room to accommodate my bowls and me, he told me. I had seventy-two bowls in that kitchen. Remember, Reader, I lived alone. I bought two more last week, too – ostensibly for a wedding present for a friend, but, alas, she's not getting them, I am.

How to make berry ice cream

This recipe is utterly fool-proof. You heat a lot of fruit with a lot of sugar, the juice of an orange and a lemon, then, when the berries start to release their juices and the sugar has dissolved, you sieve it and mix it with plenty of thick cream (which I sometimes whip just a little and sometimes, if the cream is thick enough, don't). Then you chuck it in the ice cream machine for it to work its magic, until it looks done. The only hard bit is sieving all the gently cooked fruit, which frankly is quite an effort.

When I am making a huge batch (which always seems to be on a Friday night in preparation for Le Weekend) I fill a stockpot with berries and cook them very gently, often straight from frozen. Then I take the pot, a sturdy fine-meshed sieve, a large glass bowl and myself to a prime position in front of the TV to embark on the sieving. There are some kitchen chores when the radio just doesn't cut it.

You judge the best proportion of berries to sugar by tasting (more redcurrants in the mix, for example, leads to more sugar, but more raspberries to less). If I'm using roughly a kilo of berries (a fine mixture of **raspberries**, **blackcurrants**, **redcurrants** and **blackberries**), I'll usually use about 400g **sugar** and 500ml of **double cream**, plus the juice of a **lemon** and an **orange**.

If it tastes too tart, add some more sugar. If you like it particularly creamy, use more cream; fruitier and more sorbet-like, then less. But either way, as long as it isn't bitter, people will love it. It is also a wonderful rich colour. It is especially good served with a berry compote, and I sometimes dot the 'i's and cross the 't's and put a berry jelly, made from the compote juices, on the plate, as well. Some might say this is too much of a good thing, but not in our house.

A quick summer lunch for one

A note about farro

You need to have already cooked the farro for this to be a quick lunch. Farro is a grain not unlike spelt, but with a firmer, chewier texture, and to my mind a better flavour. I often prepare a big bowl of it at the beginning of the week, so that I can throw a salad like this together in minutes, or add it to beef up a soup. It's easy to prepare, but needs soaking in plenty of water overnight. Once soaked, drain it and put into a large saucepan full of water. Bring the water to the boil, then turn the heat down and simmer for about two hours. Once cooked, let it cool in the water, which it will continue to absorb.

This is what I had for lunch on a wet August day. It took me five minutes – less even – to prepare. You need three large, juicy, delicious **tomatoes**, quartered, cored and seeded and sliced into large bite-sized chunks. (This is why this has to be a late-August lunch; the tomatoes must be mouth-wateringly delicious.) I flung these into a bowl and added the usuals: torn **basil**, **Maldon salt** and a couple of glugs of good **olive oil**. To this I added a large scoop of **farro** that had been cooking that morning, some crumbled **feta** cheese, half a **cucumber**, sliced on the diagonal into chunks a bit bigger than the tomatoes. You need a bigger bite of the cuke than the tom, it being the subtler – never say bland – partner. I dressed it with a very little **balsamic vinegar**, which I rarely use, but its sweetness is perfect here, and more oil. Always more oil. And more salt. And **black pepper**.

Afterwards, I had a chunk of almond chocolate. There is a trick to chocolate: eat your chosen chunk – a row, say – and when you have finished it, stop. My inclination is to keep going, preferably until I've finished the whole bar. It will be delicious, but the feelings of regret sour the pleasure, and there is nothing you can do about it. It sits in your stomach like a bar of soap. The hard bit is the overwhelming yearning for more than a row as you finish your last bite. But that is chocolate for you: a teasing, druggy, grabby bitch. Don't give in. The chasms of yearning stop. They really do. Your body's good sense will soon kick in, if you allow it. It has taken me 35 years to learn this.

Meat at any point?

'Meat?' Nick will inquire. 'Meat at any point?' Sometimes, in summer, I forget about meat. In autumn and winter I cook stews, braise meat and roast joints, but in summer I have to remind myself about meat, and to haul out the barbeque in order to slap on a steak that's been marinating in the fridge overnight, or a leg of lamb, some burgers, sausages or a spatchcocked lemony chicken. We also eat lots of sardines and mackerel (there are too many of us in Somerset to buy sea bass or turbot or halibut, whereas in London when I'm cooking for two, those treats seem more appropriate). Clams I buy often, too, though rarely, though for no particular reason, mussels.

But that's the thing about cooking: you develop a few dishes and particular flavours that you like working with. I'd hate to be without spices, but I'd sacrifice them for fresh herbs if push came to shove, and I cook more racks of lamb than legs or shoulders, for example, partly because I enjoy eating the tender cutlets so much and partly because, though I like eating lamb that has been slow roasted for a very long time and falls off the bone, I prefer it pink and juicy. Not that a leg of lamb can't be pink and juicy too, which means it's more about habit than anything else.

Habits should be broken. Before I met Nick, if I was cooking a bird then that bird was a chicken. But he comes back from the farmers' market in the autumn and winter bearing pheasant and quail and guinea fowl, and, as well as the pleasure of using something that has come off the land at the right time, I have discovered how much I like eating and cooking these different tasting and textured birds.

Pheasant and chorizo casserole

Pheasant has less fat on its bones than most other meats, and so suits being pot-roasted or cooked in a casserole. It can also handle robust flavours, though you don't want to cloak its distinctive 'wild' flavour. Pheasant works well in this recipe, as it stands up to the chorizo that cooks alongside it. This is one of Nick's favourite meals and, with rice and a green salad, it makes a perfectly formed winter dinner for two. It also works well for a winter party if you double or triple the amounts. If you do this, make sure that the pan is wider as well as taller than when cooking for two, as the pheasant needs to be cooked gently rather than boiled, which is what would happen in a tall pan. This is a wonderful recipe handed down from chef to chef to me, via Rory O'Connell. Originally, it came from a wonderful cook with the excellent name of George Gossip.

Joint (or ask you butcher to do it for you) a **pheasant** into eight pieces. Cut up 200g of **streaky bacon** (it's the fat you are after) into half-inch slices or lardons, and the same amount of **chorizo** into chunky bite-sized slices. I also remove the chorizo's thin skin, once it is sliced up. Slice an **onion** into half-moon rings, and peel two cloves of **garlic**. The garlic doesn't need slicing.

Heat two tablespoons of **olive oil** in a casserole dish or large saucepan that has a lid, and add the bacon. Make sure that the bacon gets coated in the oil and let it cook until its fat turns golden. Remove the bacon using a slotted spoon, so that the fat and oil are left in the pan. Place the bacon to one side.

Add the pheasant pieces to the hot fat, season them with **salt** and freshly ground **black pepper** and let them cook over the heat. Do this in batches, so that the meat seals, rather than simmers and braises.

Once the pheasant is sealed all over take the meat out of the pot and keep it to one side with the bacon. Add the onion and garlic to the pot, then put the lid on, lower the heat, and let them sweat gently until the onions are tender. Add the chorizo slices and a 400g tin of **tomatoes**, a pinch of **sugar** and two teaspoons of **smoked sweet paprika**. Cook for about ten minutes, so that you get a rich tomato sauce.

Return the pheasant and bacon to the pot. It will look like there isn't enough juice for everything to cook in, but there is. Put the lid on the casserole and cook gently for about 25 minutes, until the pheasant is cooked through. You can do this either on top of the hob or in a lowish oven (about 150°C/300°F/gas mark 2). If you think the sauce is too thick once it is done, you can always thin it with a little water or chicken stock. Serve it sprinkled with some chopped **flat-leaf parsley**.

Another meat-based meal (perfect for a lover returning late)

My friend Gordon spends at least half his life in Tangier, where he has a house and to which he generously invites his friends to stay. The flight to Tangier from London arrives very late, but when you finally make it into Gordon's house, often well after midnight, you are greeted with a small plate of meatballs in tomato sauce made by his cook Hafida. Hafida used to work for a French diplomat, so, as well as making wonderful Moroccan food, she can also turn out a fine pastry-crust and a weightless cheese soufflé. I used to think that the perfect late night meal after a journey was an omelette or a bowl of soup. But it's not; it's Hafida's meatballs. Last time I stayed with Gordon, I asked Hafida to show me how she makes them.

Hafida's meatballs

It's all very well watching Hafida mix her mince, but one of the reasons her meatballs taste so delicious is because Anour, who runs Gordon's house, has been to the butcher moments before she starts cooking. This is a crucial mince tip: raw mince deteriorates quickly, which makes sense when you think how much of the meat is exposed. It looses its freshness and flavour minute by minute. This is why you should always cook your meatballs – or burgers, or whatever – on the same day that you get your meat minced. That's another thing: try to get it minced in front of you. If you buy it ready prepared, how do you know how long it's been sitting around for? More pressure: this recipe uses raw onion and garlic so cook the meatballs within an hour of preparing and shaping them, otherwise the onion and garlic will begin to 'cook' the meat.

Take your mince (500g of minced **lamb** or **beef** will feed four for a main course or more for a late-night snack) and mix it with an **onion**, grated on a fine grater or microplane (I bought a microplane for Hafida, but as far as I can see it's never been used), a clove of **garlic**, crushed into a paste with a little **Maldon salt** against the blade of a knife, medium-sized bunches of finely chopped **coriander** and **parsley**, half a teaspoon each of **cinnamon** and **cumin** and a quarter of a teaspoon of ground **ginger**. Season with **salt** and freshly ground **black pepper**, and mix the whole lot up with your hands, so that all your goodies infiltrate every bit of mince. As your mince is so fresh you can taste your mixture before cooking it to see if it needs more of anything. (But if you'd rather not try raw mince, fry a little of it in olive and taste that.)

Meanwhile, have your tomato sauce on the go, by putting about a kilo of fresh, very ripe and delicious **tomatoes**, that have been skinned and chopped, into a large saucepan with about three tablespoons of olive oil. If it's not summer or you don't live in Morocco, use a large 800g can of Italian peeled plum tomatoes instead. Keep these on a low heat so that the tomatoes soften, then add at least three fresh red **chillies**, seeded and finely chopped, a small bunch of finely chopped **parsley**, half a teaspoon each of **cumin** and **cinnamon**, and about a teaspoon of **cayenne pepper**.

You can make this sauce earlier, of course, or just keep it gently simmering while you form the mince mixture into small balls – each one about the size of a walnut, or smaller or larger if you want. Either way, make sure the tomato sauce is gently bubbling before you drop the meatballs into it. Then add enough water so that the meatballs are *just* covered. Be careful here – you don't want to thin out your sauce too much. Keep the pot simmering for about half an hour, until the meatballs are cooked and the water has reduced.

Inevitably, the second time you make this dish it will be better than the first, because you'll understand your sauce, its consistency and tastiness. The good news is that this dish will always be delicious even if you, as Cook, note that next time you might add less water or more chilli.

Christmas

Cut to winter. Boxing day to be precise. Roast gammon and leeks, potato dauphinoise and red cabbage. This is everyone's favourite winter meal in our house, and it is a cinch to run up because nothing much has to happen at the last minute except sautéing the leeks. I even make the red cabbage the day before, which sounds fine, but the day before Boxing Day is Christmas Day when there is more than enough to do already. And yet it all gets done. I try not to get grumpy while cooking, but I sometimes do. I believe firmly that there is no place for the martyr in the kitchen, and, after all, if my parents only taught me one lesson about cooking, it was that I, as a young woman, did not have to do it – at least no more than is necessary to lead a civilised life.

I cook because I enjoy it, but occasionally I forget this and I become a weird, freaky, control person *who has to do everything*. I forget that when people offer to help they actually want to help, not be turned away. They want to eat something that has been made in a relaxed way by many hands, rather

than by a single someone banging saucepans, getting stressed and clearly feeling put upon.

To this end, now, when one of us – usually Ron who grows all the vegetables – collects a bucket full of leeks from the icy garden, I give them a good wash, collect up knives and people, issue instructions about very thin slivery slices, turn the radio on, and marvel at the speed and good humour of collective effort. We eat leeks cooked like this every day around Christmas, which means there is always a lot of chopping. This dish is a winter version of the summer broad bean medley hit.

Boxing Day leeks with spinach and peas

How straightforward is this? Wash the **leeks**. Slice them very finely. Heat two or three tablespoons of **olive oil** in a sauté or deep frying pan, then, once hot, add your leeks. Let them cook for about eight to ten minutes in the oil, giving them a stir every now and then. Meanwhile, boil some water in a smaller saucepan and add a load of frozen **peas**. The mixture is best with a ratio of about one-third peas to two-thirds leeks, but this is not a moment when precision is important. Chop two good handfuls of **flat-leaf parsley**. Give the leeks another stir. Gather some spinach – **baby spinach** is best for this – and give it a wash, then dry it. Once the leeks are cooked, season them with **Maldon salt**, freshly ground **black pepper** and a tiny squeeze of **lemon juice** (you don't want to taste the lemon, just for it to lift the other flavours). Add the parsley, then tip the leeks, oil and all, out of the sauté pan into a large bowl. Drain the peas once they are cooked and add them to the leeks. Add the spinach, too. It will wilt to the perfect degree from the heat of the other vegetables.

You might also add a few strips of **bacon** to the pan and cook it for a while before adding the leeks. This can make a very good meal by itself. But on Boxing Day this will not do. On Boxing Day you have to eat a very great deal. It's the law.

Roast gammon

Although most modern brining uses less salt than it once did, it is still a good idea to soak the gammon in a large saucepan of cold water for 24 hours to get rid of any excess salt. If you don't have time to do this then bring a pan of water to the boil – with the gammon in it – simmer for two minutes then drain.

To cook the **gammon**, preheat the oven to 160°C/325°F/gas mark 3. A 2.75kg joint will feed eight to ten people easily. I like to cook it pretty simply, using a classic honey, clove and mustard coating. You want to roast it covered, and the best way to do this is to create an aluminium-foil package for it within a large roasting tray. Use two large sheets of foil laid out, one across the other, in a tray in a cross shape, put the gammon in the middle, bring up the edges of the foil and fold them together, so that the package is airtight but loose around the meat, so that the hot air has room to circulate. Roast the gammon for two hours. Take it out after this time, and then turn up the oven to 220°C/425°F/gas mark 7.

Lift the gammon out of the roasting tray and put it on a large chopping board. What you have to do now is remove its skin and the fat that comes away with the skin – it comes away pretty easily if you make a couple of long cuts across the skin, without letting your knife cut deep into the fat. Then just pull it off using your hands, though wear rubber gloves or use a tea towel to protect them from the hot fat. (I keep a box of surgeon's gloves in the kitchen for jobs like this.)

Once you have removed the skin you will still be left with a layer of fat and it is this layer that you want to crisp up and cover with a glaze. Mix a couple of tablespoons of grainy **Dijon mustard** together will a couple more generous tablespoons of clear **honey** and smear it all over the joint using your hands. Some will drip down and that's fine, just keep smearing it back on; enough will stick. Now cut a criss-cross diamond pattern all over the fat using a sharp knife and push a **clove** into the centre of each diamond. Put the joint back in the hot oven for another twenty-five minutes or so – so that it cooks until the glaze has turned a rich brown colour.

Let it rest for twenty minutes with a bit of foil draped carefully over it before slicing it, or, if you prefer, let it cool completely and serve it cold.

Braised red cabbage

Preheat the oven to 140°C/275°F/gas mark 1. Trim one beautiful **red cabbage** of its outer tough leaves, cut it into quarters and trim away the core. Shred it into thin slices either in a food processor or by hand. Put it into a large casserole that has a well-fitting lid. Add 200ml of **malt vinegar** (it is the flavour of cheap malt vinegar that you are after here, rather than a more refined wine vinegar), 50ml of water, 100g of **Demerara sugar**, 125g of **butter**, cut into cubes, and a teaspoon of **Maldon salt**. Crush about twelve **juniper berries** in a pestle and mortar or spice grinder and add them, along with a single whole **star anise**, to the cabbage. Give everything a stir. Put the lid on the casserole or saucepan or cover securely with aluminium foil and put it into the oven for three hours.

Half way through the cooking time, take the casserole out of the oven and give the whole thing another good stir. Once the cabbage is done, check the seasoning and, if you can find it easily enough, throw away the star anise. I almost always cook the cabbage the day before serving it, and then re-heat it slowly on the hob the next day.

Potatoes dauphinoise

Potatoes dauphinoise is named after the wintry Alpine region of France, the Dauphiné, from where the dish originates. As this would imply, a dish of potatoes dauphinoise is the perfect winter comfort food. It should be crispy and golden brown on top and creamy and soft when you push your spoon inside.

This is easy to do if you use an earthenware or Pyrex gratin dish, which can be any shape, and as large or small as you have people to feed. What is more important is depth, and a dish about 6cm deep is ideal. The dish needs to be **buttered** around its bottom and sides liberally – a layer rather than a smear. Preheat the oven to 160°C/325°F/gas mark 3. Now slice your potatoes. Use waxy **potatoes**, and peel them first. It doesn't matter what size they are as long as the slices are more or less the same width, and that width is thin. I use a mandolin, which does the job quickly and effortlessly. How many potatoes? As many as fill the dish you are using, leaving a space of about a centimetre at the top. Now chop some **garlic** very finely. For a large gratin dish that will feed about ten people I chop about four fat cloves of garlic.

I once made potato dauphinoise when I was cross and as a result of my irritation I grew careless and over salted the potatoes. This was a shame and, as a result I now always season the cream first, which means I can taste it before adding the potatoes. This also means the flavours merge together better.

So, to feed ten people pour 900ml of double (though single is fine, too) **cream** into a large bowl and add the chopped up garlic, **Maldon salt** and freshly ground **black pepper**. Mix everything together well and taste it to check the seasoning is correct. (If it's too salty, add more cream.) Once the cream is ready, put the slices of potato into the bowl, and, using your hands to mix everything together, make sure each slice is well covered in cream.

Fill the buttery gratin dish with the creamy potatoes. The potato slices don't have to be in any neat order, but make sure that all the slices are lying flat and not sticking up. Pour any scrapings of cream from the bowl over the top of the potatoes.

Bake in the oven for about an hour and a half, though start glancing at it after an hour and a quarter. It will be done when it is just bubbling and beginning to brown on top. I usually put it under the grill for a few minutes to really brown and crisp up the top, but if you do this you have to watch it and whip it out as soon as it is golden. Otherwise, it is a good-natured dish and once cooked can be left in a low oven while you attend to other bits of the meal.

This takes us back to the leeks. It takes me back to their being chopped by Nick or one of my sisters or brothers-in-law or by a visiting friend; back to the half hour we have spent talking in the warm kitchen together; back to their being grown and picked by Ron, in a garden created by my mum and dad, a garden where their small grandchildren now plant their own red radishes, courgettes and carrots, and which I hope one day to teach them to cook.

My happy ending

I found a little note-to-self in one of my notebooks not long ago, obviously written in a moment of yearning self-pity.

I want a garden with scented geraniums growing in it and all that that implies, the note read. I'd clearly just eaten poached plums or blackberry compote scented with geranium leaves, and after the sugar high had worn off had indulged in a private hissy fit. A garden with geraniums and all that that implies? Well, I think we can deduce that it implies a house attached to said garden, and a nice partner somewhere about the place to share it all with – pruning the plum tree, preferably. I'd even cook him scented compotes if only he'd just bloody show up. Not much to ask for then, as a freelance journalist, single, living in London.

Talk about putting it out there. Because guess what? Not long after talking about living together, Nick and I found a house – on the Internet, the way you do – and the house has a garden and in the garden is a mulberry tree, two apple trees, a blackberry bush, two elders and a greengage tree. Bring on the scented geraniums.

Bibliography

Seemingly, I'm obsessive about buying cookery books. I read them, look at them and use them a great deal. Even so, there is no doubt that I have acquired more than I need.

'But I collect them,' I say to Nick when he looks aghast at some further addition. Saying such a thing makes me blush. I don't think of myself as a collector of anything, but somehow the books, like the bowls, have piled up.

'It's time to stop,' Nick said to me firmly when I came home one afternoon feeling triumphant with my latest find: a battered old copy of *The Gold and Fizdale Cookbook*, a fabulous book by a New York couple, Arthur Gold and Robert Fizdale – professional duo pianists no less, who began writing about food after they cooked a Moroccan feast for their pal Julia Child (this was in the '70s, in Long Island, New York, when Moroccan feasts weren't served up every night of the week), and she insisted that they pursue a second career.

'You don't need any more cookbooks,' Nick continued, 'so just stop. Stop.' He sounded firm and exasperated. Nick doesn't need garb of any kind to perk himself up, whereas buying a bag of golden sultanas, never mind a second-hand cookbook, can transform my day.

'You're right,' I said to him, and resolved to do better. So when a couple of weeks later, as one of my Christmas presents, he gave me *1080 Recipes* by Simone and Inés Ortega – as big a cookery book as you can buy – I thought: God love him, this is a man resigned to his lot.

I simply can't list the many cookbooks that have been meaningful to me over the years, but instead, below, cite the books that have been especially helpful in teaching me to cook and cook better.

Ballymaloe Cookery Course
Darina Allen
(Kyle Cathie, 2007)

This is my 'bible' cookbook. I refer to it almost daily. It's primarily a teaching book and the recipes are honed from years of constant scrutiny, which means that they are pretty much perfect, as well as clear and full of explanation. Every single one is a keeper. It will tell you how to butterfly a leg of lamb and how to cook it, but also about the way lamb changes over a season, and how it is delicious served with crusty potatoes, a green salad, apple and mint jelly or apple and tomato chutney – and how to make all those things, too.

Mastering the Art of French Cooking
Julia Child
(Random House USA, 2001)

For the chocolate soufflé recipe alone, *Volume One* of this consummate work is worth buying. And the brilliance of the soufflé recipe – how it actually works, how its instructions are so precisely laid out, so that there is no room for confusion – holds true for much of the rest of the book and *Volume Two*, too.

An Omelette and a Glass of Wine and
Is There a Nutmeg in the House?
Elizabeth David
(Penguin Books Ltd, 1990, 2001)

It's Elizabeth David. What more can one say? Her books more than live up to her reputation. Her more conventional recipe books – *French Provincial Cooking*, for instance – are of course masterful, but I find these two anthologies – compiled from her articles, letters, files and notes – even more useful, because her voice, and believe me it's her voice you want in your ear in the kitchen, comes across even more directly. Reading about Elizabeth David fretting about transporting partridges with lentils to a friend's kitchenless flat (only that of André Simon) for a dinner party, is more of an invitation to cook such a dish, than having to find the recipe among many others. And in *Is There a Nutmeg in the House?* there is a chapter entitled Do not Despair over Rice. When you are learning to cook it doesn't get any better than that.

The Oxford Companion to Food
Alan Davidson
(Oxford University Press, 2006)
Michael gave me this book. It's a comprehensive reference book, scholarly yet accessible. You can look up anything you're not sure about or want more information on. The longer essays – on fish, say, or dates or noodles – are great reads, as well as packed with useful information.

The River Café Cook Book, River Café Cook Book Two, River Café Cook Book Green, River Café Cook Book Easy, River Café Two Easy
Rose Gray and Ruth Rogers
(Ebury Press 1996, 1998, 2001, 2003, 2005)
Every one of these books is inspired; full of things that you want to eat so, so, so much. They are classic wonderful recipes – grilled squid with chilli and rocket, chocolate nemesis, pork cooked in milk, *pappa al pomodoro*, penne with sausage sauce. Also, the more you cook from the River Café books the better you will understand the ingredients you are using – the effect of garlic, for example, the taste of herbs, what Parmesan does to a dish, and so on.

Jane Grigson's Vegetable Book
Jane Grigson
(Penguin Books Ltd, 1998)
To pick up any book by Jane Grigson is to be seduced and want to cook. Gift enough. The first recipe I followed from this book was for Greek stewed green beans. I remembered eating them in Corfu when I was eighteen, wondered where I would find how to reproduce that magic dish, picked up Jane Grigson, and there it was, explained simply and precisely. On the following page is Grigson's fantastic Soupe au Pistou recipe, complete with a description of Tours's annual garlic and basil fair.

The Classic Italian Cookbook
Marcella Hazan
(Papermac, 1981)
When I was watching people cook in New York, I longed to be able to run up pasta with garlic and olive oil. It was, everyone said, the simplest recipe in the world. Oh yeah? For the novice cook it's the sort of dish which makes you loose your nerve. When I first tried it, either the garlic went funny on me (read burnt), or the whole dish tasted bland. This book teaches you how to make the simplest dishes properly: this one, braised fennel, potato gnocchi, as well as some spectaculars: baked seabass stuffed with mussels, shrimps and oysters, just for example.

Fish etc.
Mark Hix
(Quadrille Publishing Ltd, 2004)
This book tells you how to store fish, fillet it, prepare it and cook it. But lots of fish books do that. This one also has the best actual recipes, to my mind – for anything from fish

pie and kedgeree, to tempura prawns and herring salad as well as how to grill, poach, fry, steam and roast fish in myriad ways.

Roast Chicken and Other Stories
Simon Hopkinson
(Ebury Press, 1999)

No surprise here. Wonderful recipes, of course, but what Hopkinson also does is make you think more, and more creatively about ingredients. He is a stickler in the very best sense, and teaches the reader to be so, too.

Made in Italy
Giorigo Locatelli
(Fourth Estate, 2008)

An extravagant book, but not pointlessly so. It's as useful as it is beautiful, with the best explanation for making risotto that I've ever read. It's wonderful on Italian ingredients, too, with whole pages on prosciutto, ricotta and chicory, as well as fantastic recipes, photographs and stories.

Cooking with Pomiane
Edouard de Pomiane
(Random House USA Inc, 2001)

This book was published in France in the 1930s, but reads as if it was written yesterday and, as far as I'm concerned, especially for me. Listen to Pomiane's explanation of how to fry potatoes: "Can one fry whole potatoes, you ask? No, because at this high temperature the surface will brown quickly whilst the inside remains raw. Hence the second rule for frying: only fry food in small pieces." The whole book is like that. Plus recipes. And folklore. And poetry. And history. And humour. And how to make gravy.

The Book of Jewish Food
Claudia Roden
(Penguin Books Ltd, 1999)

Claudia Roden isn't a chef; she's an historian, storyteller and reporter as well. This book is a masterpiece. It contains a history of Judaism, takes in the food of Eastern Europe, North Africa, New York, Israel, India, Spain, Turkey, Ethiopia, Georgia and the Middle East, and is as much about migration, tradition, family, community and lore, as it is about food. It also insists that you cook using your common sense and your own sense of taste – always a good lesson.

Appetite
Nigel Slater
(Fourth Estate, 2001)

When I began cooking in London, I used this book endlessly, and the only reason I don't now is because I know so many of the recipes by heart. This is the book that I would buy anyone just starting to cook (which is not to preclude it from anyone more experienced). It is full of recipes that you will use over and over again and will begin to adapt: a winter soup with dried beans, a supper dish of chicken with garlic and herbs, sausages and mash with a really good onion gravy, a fabulous chocolate cake. All Nigel Slater's books are great, though this is still my favourite.

Bread Matters
Andrew Whitley
(Fourth Estate, 2006)

If you want to bake bread, this is the book you need. I got to grips with sourdough bread – no mean feat, quite frankly – using this book.

Acknowledgements I would like to thank Clare Lattin. Without her, this book wouldn't exist. Nor would it without Michael Austin, on whose boat I learnt to cook and who was the dreamiest, funniest, most fabulous skipper on the planet, and what's more a very good cook. I think of my boat mates on that crossing – Jeremy Grosvenor, Toby Corbett and David Fletcher – often. They looked after me so well in every way.

Rose Gray, Nell Campbell and Bess Rattray all taught me, early on, about the pleasures of cooking in general, as well as how to cook many things more specifically. So, too, has Rory O'Connell. It is his recipes that I turn to most often, and I use many of them in this book. David Nicholls, Aurore Papafava, Canice Sharkey, Thomas Dane, Gordon Watson, Katrine Boorman, Danny Moynihan, Victoria Fernandez, John David Rhodes and Joanna Weinberg are all constant sources of cooking inspiration, as was Peter Kent. Tim Allen taught me how to make bread. Ron Garrett grows all the vegetables in Somerset, which is only a part of what he does daily and nightly for all of us, as does Jo Garrett. I owe them all huge thank yous. I owe a huge debt of gratitude to all the other cooks and writers whose recipes I use in this book as well as in my kitchen: Ruth Rogers, Mark Hix, Simon Hopkinson, Annie Bell, Sally Clarke, Kyle Canepa, Bess Rattray, Una Hanley, Hafida Ben Drissd, Margarita Barila, Saskia Spender and Jackie Sohier.

I have been lucky in having an incredibly patient and meticulous editor, Laura Herring, and a publisher, Jane O'Shea, who couldn't have been more encouraging. I thank Carmen Carreira for her wonderful illustrations and Claire Peters for designing the book so beautifully.

But it is the people with whom I eat most often that I owe the most thanks: Polly, Andy, Rose and Bay Garnett, Tom, George and Frankie Browne, Tom and Billy Craig, Nicholas, Kit and Lulu Pearson.

42 'Spaghetti with squid and courgette' reprinted by permission from Rose Gray and Ruth Rogers and adapted from *River Café Two Easy*, published by Ebury Press.

88-9 'Souffle au chocolat' from *Mastering the Art of French Cooking, Vol. 1* by Julia Child, Louisette Bertholle and Simone Beck, copyright © 1961 by Alfred A. Knopf, a division of Random House, Inc. Used by permission of Alfred A. Knopf, a division of Random House, Inc.

99-100 'Sesame beef salad' adapted from *Leith's Cookery Bible* by Prue Leith and Caroline Waldegrave, published by Bloomsbury Publishing Plc. Reprinted by permission of PFD on behalf of Leith's School of Food and Wine. ©: as printed in the original volume.

101 'Fish stock' and **102-3** 'Fish pie' reprinted by permission from Mark Hix and adapted from *Fish etc.*, published by Quadrille.

108-9 'Tomato and basil lasagne' adapted from *Living and Eating* by Annie Bell and John Pawson, published by Ebury. Reprinted by permission of the Random House Group Ltd.

133 'Strawberry sorbet' reprinted by permission from Rose Gray and Ruth Rogers and adapted from *The River Café Cook Book*, published by Ebury Press.

148-9 'Tarte Tatin' from *Sally Clarke's Book* by Sally Clarke. Reprinted by permission from Grub Street Publishing.

161 'Scallop and artichoke soup' from *Roast Chicken and Other Stories* by Simon Hopkinson, published by Ebury Press. Reprinted by permission from David Higham Associates Limited.

194 'Lemony pork chops' reprinted by permission from Rose Gray and Ruth Rogers and adapted from *River Café Cook Book Easy*, published by Ebury Press.